Table of Contents

References

Sculpting Sanctity

Talent and Time in the Service of God

by

Dr. ant

Although the author and publisher have made every effort to ensure that the information in this book was correct at press time, the author and publisher do not assume and hereby disclaim any liability to any party for any loss, damage, or disruption caused by errors or omissions, whether such errors or omissions result from negligence, accident, or any other cause.

This publication is designed to provide accurate and authoritative information with regard to the subject matter covered. It is sold with the understanding that the publisher is not engaged in rendering professional services. If legal advice or other expert assistance is required, the services of a competent professional should be sought.

The fact that an organization or website is referred to in this work as a citation and/or a potential source of further information does not mean that the author or the publisher endorses the information the organization or website may provide or recommendations it may make.

Please remember that Internet websites listed in this work may have changed or disappeared between when this work was written and when it is read.

Sculpting Sanctity: Talent and Time in the Service of God

Contents

Embracing the Catholic Imagination

The intersection of faith and creativity forms the bedrock of what we term the Catholic Imagination—a boundless vista where the divine intertwines with the human, where the eternal brushes against the temporal. This sacred imagination is not merely a faculty of the mind but an invitation to participate in a reality that transcends our physical world. It is in this space that art enthusiasts, Roman Catholics, art professors and students alike are called to explore and contribute to a legacy that mirrors the vastness and depth of Catholic thought and culture.

At the heart of the Catholic Imagination lies the profound recognition of creation as a cooperative act with the Divine. Every stroke of the painter's brush, every chisel mark on stone, and every note in a sacred hymn are seen as participations in God's continuous act of creation. The artistic endeavors that spring from this well of inspiration are not mere expressions of human creativity but are imbued with the potential to be conduits of grace. This perspective challenges the modern separation of the secular from the sacred, inviting a holistic view of talent as a gift to be oriented towards the glorification of God and the sanctification of the world.

Understanding the eternal import of Catholic art necessitates a journey through history, theology, and the realms of the spirit. It is a journey that reveals how Catholic art is not confined to the decorative or the purely aesthetic but is deeply integrated into the fabric of faith itself. The sacramental vision of reality that characterizes Catholic thought perceives the world as imbued with God's grace, accessible through signs and symbols. This sacramentality is the fertile ground in which the Catholic Imagination flourishes, weaving together the visible and the invisible into a tapestry of divine revelation.

The role of talent within this divine economy is both a privilege and a responsibility. To possess a talent is to acknowledge a gift from God, intended not for personal glorification but as a means of drawing oneself and others closer to the transcendent truth. The utilization of talent in service to God's glory becomes an act of worship, a doxology that elevates the natural into the realm of the supernatural.

The conception of time itself is transformed in the light of the Catholic Imagination. Rather than a mere succession of moments, time becomes the canvas upon which God's redemptive work is unveiled. The liturgical calendar structures time in such a way that every moment holds the potential for an encounter with the divine, offering a framework for creativity that is intrinsically oriented towards the eschatological horizon.

Within this sacred temporality, the symphony of Catholic art—encompassing visual arts, music, literature, philosophy, theology, and even the scientific quest for understanding—finds its deepest resonance. Each modality of artistic expression is a reflection of the infinite beauty of God, an echo of the harmony that underlies creation.

The legacy of Catholic art is rich and diverse, stretching from the catacombs of the early Church to the masterpieces of the Renaissance, and beyond into the modern era. This continuity and evolution of artistic expression highlight the Church's ongoing dialogue with culture, a dialogue that seeks to reveal the luminous face of Christ to every generation.

The saints, as the masterpieces of God's grace, embody the ultimate realization of the Catholic Imagination. Their lives, marked by holiness and artistic creativity, serve as both inspiration and intercession for those who seek to consecrate their talents to the divine. Patron saints of the arts, in particular, exemplify the integration of artistic excellence and sanctity, pointing the way for artists to live out their vocation within the heart of the Church.

Moreover, the integration of science and faith within the Catholic worldview dispels the myth of an inherent conflict between the two. Catholic scientists throughout history have contributed to human knowledge while deepening their understanding of the created order as a reflection of the Creator. This holistic view fosters an art that is both true and beautiful, grounded in a reality that transcends the empirical.

The moral dimension of Catholic art challenges artists to navigate the complexities of human existence with integrity and compassion. Art becomes a medium through which ethical dilemmas are explored and the dignity of the human person is affirmed. This engagement with the moral imagination is a critical aspect of the Catholic artist's contribution to the world.

Politics and the Catholic conscience are also deeply intertwined with the vocation of the Catholic artist. Artistic expressions of justice and peace serve as prophetic voices within society, calling attention to the demands of the Gospel in the public square. Through their work, Catholic artists participate in the Church's mission of social transformation, inspired by the principles of Catholic social teaching.

Education and formation through beauty reveal another dimension of the Catholic Imagination. Art, in its ability to convey truth through beauty, becomes an essential pathway for spiritual and intellectual growth. The role of art in Catholic education underscores the importance of cultivating an aesthetic sensibility alongside moral and intellectual virtues.

The mission and evangelization efforts of the Church are enriched by the Catholic Imagination, which views art as a universal language capable of bridging cultural and linguistic divides. Through artistic expression, the Gospel message is incarnated anew, inviting encounter and dialogue with the world.

In the creation of sacred spaces, whether through architecture, liturgy, or the visual and performing arts, the Catholic Imagination seeks to facilitate encounters with the divine. These spaces, both physical and metaphorical, are designed to draw the faithful into a deeper communion with God, serving as thresholds to the sacred.

Finally, the Catholic Imagination is both a heritage to be received and a mission to be lived. It invites artists to see themselves as prophets and pilgrims, journeying towards the fullness of truth and beauty in God. In embracing the Catholic Imagination, artists participate in the ongoing work of salvation, education, and conversion, cooperating with God's grace to reveal glimpses of heaven on earth.

Chapter 1: The Essence of Catholic Creativity

Catholic creativity, in its most profound form, intertwines with the divine, acting as a conduit through which the celestial and the terrestrial realms communicate. This unique form of creativity doesn't just emanate from human talent or intellectual pursuit; it is, at its core, a divine collaboration. The essence of Catholic creativity lies in its ability to render the invisible God visible, to make the intangible grace of the Creator tangible through human works of art, literature, and architecture. This chapter aims to unravel the sacred intertwining of divine grace and human creativity, illuminating how this synergy has shaped history, theology, and culture within the Catholic tradition.

At the heart of Catholic creativity is the concept of sacramentality. This sacramental worldview perceives the whole of creation as a manifestation of God's grace, where every element of the natural world, every human articulation, can potentially serve as a visible sign of an invisible reality. This profound understanding has inspired countless artists, architects, writers, and musicians throughout the ages to attempt to capture a glimpse of the divine mystery. They engage not just in artistic creation but in a form of prayer, a deeply spiritual act that seeks to echo the work of the Creator himself (Vatican II, Sacrosanctum Concilium, 1963).

Historically, Catholic creativity has traversed through epochs, each leaving an indelible mark on the fabric of human civilization. From the clandestine symbols etched into the walls of the Roman catacombs, serving as secret codes of faith during times of persecution, to the majestic opulence of the Renaissance, where art became a divine portal to the sacred. These periods illustrate not merely the evolution of artistic skill but the unyielding resilience and adaptability of Catholic imagination in echoing the divine across centuries.

The theological foundations of Catholic creativity, deeply rooted in the Incarnation, manifest God's ultimate act of creativity—becoming man. This mystery underscores the belief in the inherent goodness of the material world and the body, against the dualistic tendencies that denigrate the physical in favor of the spiritual. It is this conviction that has propelled Catholic artists to embrace the material world as a stage for divine encounter, transforming stone, pigment, and sound into conduits of spiritual experience and conveyors of theological truth (John Paul II, Letter to Artists, 1999).

In essence, Catholic creativity is a testament to the human capacity to transcend the ordinary, to envisage the kingdom of God within the mundane. Every authentic expression of Catholic art and thought is an act of co-creation with the Divine, a microcosm of the Creator's breath that animates the universe. As we delve into the layers of Catholic creativity, we embark on a pilgrimage through time and talent, discovering how art becomes a verb that communicates the eternal, educates the mind, converts the heart, and elevates the soul towards the ultimate Creator.

The Theological Foundations

The world of Catholic creativity is deeply rooted in theological foundations that shape its unique vision and mission. At the heart of this vision lies the understanding that creation itself is a reflection of the Creator's glory, an echo of the divine that speaks to us through beauty, form, and color. This theological underpinning is not merely an abstract concept but a living reality that infuses Catholic art with its profound sense of purpose and sanctity.

The doctrine of Imago Dei, the belief that humanity is created in the image and likeness of God, forms the bedrock of Catholic artistic expression. It imbues the act of creation with a sacred significance, for in crafting works of art, the Catholic artist participates in the divine act of creation. Each stroke of the brush, each chisel mark on stone, each note in a harmonious melody becomes an act of worship, a testament to the glory of the Creator reflected in the creativity of the human spirit.

This participation in the divine is further illuminated through the Incarnation—the Word made flesh. The Incarnation reveals that the material world is capable of bearing the divine, thus sanctifying the use of physical materials in religious art. From the luminous frescoes of the Sistine Chapel to the solemn beauty of Gregorian chant, Catholic creativity endeavors to manifest the divine mystery through material means, bridging the gap between the heavenly and the earthly.

The sacramental worldview, fundamental to Catholic theology, emphasizes that grace is transmitted through visible signs and symbols. Art, in this context, becomes a sacramental, a visible sign through which spiritual truths are conveyed. This sacramentality of art suggests that Catholic creations are not mere decorations or aesthetic pursuits; they are vessels of grace, imbued with the ability to lead the soul closer to the Divine.

Moreover, Catholic creativity is marked by a profound eschatological dimension. It points beyond itself to the ultimate reality of God's kingdom. In this sense, Catholic art is inherently teleological, oriented towards the final end, the beatific vision. Through beauty, it seeks to awaken a longing in the human heart for the divine, to stir the soul with a sense of the transcendent.

The communion of saints also plays a crucial role in shaping the theology of Catholic creativity. Saints, as exemplars of holiness, are often portrayed in Catholic art, not merely as historical figures but as participants in the eternal liturgy of heaven. Through their representation, Catholic art invites the faithful to a deeper fellowship with these holy men and women, encouraging them to emulate their virtues and to seek their intercession.

Marian devotion, too, finds its artistic expression within this theological landscape. The Blessed Virgin Mary, as the first tabernacle of the Incarnation, is venerated through countless works of art that seek to capture her purity, her humility, and her maternal care. In portraying Mary, Catholic artists not only honor the Mother of God but also reflect on her pivotal role in the salvation history.

At its core, therefore, Catholic creativity is an expression of faith, a profound dialogue between the seen and the unseen. It is an exploration of the mystery of existence, a journey that seeks to illuminate the human experience in light of divine revelation. Through its various forms—be it painting, sculpture, music, or literature—Catholic art strives to articulate the ineffable, to give voice to the whispers of the Divine that permeate our world.

In conclusion, the theological foundations of Catholic creativity underscore a vision of art that is deeply sacramental, incarnational, and eschatological. This vision challenges the Catholic artist to transcend the temporal, to craft works that reflect the eternal beauty of the divine, and to participate in the salvific mission of the Church by drawing souls closer to God through the power of beauty.

Sacramentality and Signs

In the heart of Catholic thought, the universe itself is a sacrament, a visible sign of an invisible grace. This sacred vision forms the foundation upon which the Catholic imagination thrives, engaging artists, theologians, and believers alike in a profound dialogue with the Divine through the tangible world. The essence of sacramentality lies in its ability to mediate the holy, to make the intangible graspable, and to draw the faithful into a deeper encounter with God. This mediation is not incidental but essential to the faith, revealing the incarnational nature of Christianity, where the Word took flesh and dwelt among us.

Understanding sacramentality requires an exploration of signs, symbols, and their significance within Catholic tradition. Signs, in their simplest form, point beyond themselves to a greater reality. In the context of Catholic art and thought, they are imbued with a divine purpose, serving as conduits of grace and windows to the transcendent. The sign acts, not merely as a reminder but as a real participation in the mysteries it represents. This dynamic interplay between the material and spiritual characterizes the Catholic approach to art, seeing in it not just a reflection of divine beauty but a participation in it.

Catholic art is sacramental in that it manifests the invisible through the visible, bringing the sacred to life in color, form, and sound. This sacramentality transforms churches into spaces where heaven touches earth, icons become windows to the divine, and music carries the echo of angels. The artist, in this sacred economy, becomes a co-creator with God, wielding talent as a means of grace. This vocation is not a mere profession but a call to participate in the divine act of revelation, making known the mystery of the incarnation through matter and beauty.

The concept of sacramentality extends beyond the realm of liturgical arts, permeating every facet of Catholic creativity. Literature, architecture, and even the culinary arts can be expressions of this deep sacramental understanding, revealing aspects of God's grace in the diversity of human experience. A Catholic novel, for instance, can offer insights into redemption, suffering, and the presence of grace in human affairs, inviting the reader into a deeper reflection on the mysteries of faith.

In a world increasingly dominated by the secular, the sacramental vision offers a counter-narrative that affirms the presence of the divine in the mundane. It challenges the modern dichotomy between the sacred and profane, inviting a re-enchantment of the world through a sacramental lens. This perspective sees every created thing as a potential bearer of grace, every human encounter as a site of divine revelation, and every creative act as a participation in the ongoing creation of the world.

The teaching of the Church underscores the importance of signs as means of communion with the divine. The Catechism of the

Catholic Church, for instance, describes sacraments as 'efficacious signs of grace' (Catechism of the Catholic Church, 1994). This efficaciousness highlights the active nature of sacramental signs, not only pointing to divine realities but making them present and operative in the here and now. This understanding deepens the role of the artist, who is called to create not just aesthetically pleasing works, but ones that can truly mediate grace to the viewer.

Critical to the sacramental worldview is the realization that while signs and symbols mediate the divine, they do not contain or limit the transcendent. Rather, they invite the faithful into an ever-deeper mystery, a journey towards the infinite that can never be fully encapsulated by human artistry or language. This recognition nurtures a humility in the Catholic artist, whose work becomes a form of prayer, an offering that acknowledges the greatness of God and the limitations of human expression.

The sacramental principle also fosters a deep sense of solidarity and communion, both with the Creator and with creation. In recognizing the world as charged with divine significance, the faithful are called to stewardship and love, seeing in their fellow human beings and in the whole of creation a reflection of God's glory. This has profound implications for how Catholics engage with the world, fostering an ethic of care, respect, and reverence for life in all its forms.

Moreover, sacramentality shapes the liturgical life of the Church, imbuing rites and ceremonies with deep symbolic meaning. The liturgy itself is a prime example of sacramentality at work, where bread and wine are transformed into the Body and Blood of Christ. Through these signs, the faithful participate in the Paschal Mystery, entering into the death and resurrection of Jesus. This liturgical participation is mirrored in the broader artistic vocation, where the act of creation becomes a sharing in the paschal mystery, a death to self, and a resurrection in the act of giving form to divine inspiration.

The challenges facing the Catholic artist in this sacramental endeavor are manifold. In a culture that often values the immediate and the superficial, the deep symbolism and layers of meaning inherent in sacramental art can be overlooked or misunderstood. The artist must navigate these waters with care, striving to communicate the depths of faith in a language that can be accessible without sacrificing profundity.

Moreover, the call to create sacramental art is a call to holiness, demanding authenticity of life and purity of intention. The effectiveness of sacramental signs, in part, depends on the sanctity of those who create them. An artist living in discord with the truths they seek to convey undermines the sacramental economy, severing the sign from the grace it is meant to mediate.

In conclusion, the sacramentality and signs within Catholic art and thought embody a profound theology of incarnation, where the material world becomes a means of encountering the divine. This vision challenges both artist and viewer to look beyond the surface, to see in the created world a reflection of the Creator, and to engage with art as a form of prayer and a journey into mystery. It is here, in the interplay of sign and sacrament, that the Catholic imagination finds its truest expression, inviting all into a deeper participation in the divine life.

Historical Perspectives

The exploration of Catholic creativity's essence is incomplete without a journey through its historical landscapes. From the dimly lit corridors of the catacombs, where the first Christians expressed their faith through simple symbols etched in stone, to the grandiosity of Renaissance cathedrals adorned with art that speaks of heaven on earth, a thread of divine inspiration weaves through the history of Catholic art. The progression of Catholic creativity over the centuries reflects not only the evolution of artistic techniques but also a deepening understanding of the faith and its expression in the material world.

In the early Christian community, art served as a catechetical tool, a means of instructing the faithful and conveying the truths of a religion that was often forced to remain hidden from the public eye. The images of fish, loaves, and the Good Shepherd, found in the catacombs of Rome, articulated elements of Christian belief to those who were literate in symbols rather than words. This visual theology laid the groundwork for a faith that perceives the created world as a canvas of the Creator's love and majesty.

As Christianity emerged from the catacombs, the church embraced the arts with a vision that saw beauty and truth as inextricably linked. The Byzantine era, for instance, gave birth to the iconography tradition, in which images of Christ, the Virgin Mary, and the saints were not mere decorations but windows to the divine, inviting the viewer into a contemplative encounter with the holy.

The Middle Ages further crystallized the role of art in Catholic worship and pedagogy. The grand cathedrals, with their soaring Gothic arches and stained glass, stood as sermons in stone and light, designed to lift the mind and heart to God. It was during this time that the church articulated a robust theology of sacramentality, affirming that grace could be mediated through the physical, through the tangible creations of human hands.

The Renaissance heralded a renewed emphasis on the human person's dignity and the natural world's beauty, elements deeply resonant with Catholic thought. Artists like Michelangelo and Leonardo da Vinci pursued their craft with a sense of divine calling, exploring themes of incarnation, redemption, and the human soul's aspirations. Their work, and that of their contemporaries, illustrated the Renaissance Catholic Church's belief in human creativity as a participation in the creative act of God.

This historical journey underscores the church's recognition of art's power to transcend language and culture, communicating the gospel's truths to every generation. Whether through the frescoes of Giotto, the compositions of Palestrina, or the narratives of Dante, Catholic creativity has sought to render visible the invisible, to make tangible the intangible realities of faith.

Yet, the history of Catholic art is not merely a chronology of styles and masters. It is a testament to the enduring belief that beauty has the power to open hearts to the mystery of God. Pope John Paul II, in his Letter to Artists (1999), echoed this sentiment, reminding artists of their vocation to be stewards of beauty, contributing to the renewal of culture and society.

In our contemporary age, this historical perspective invites artists and believers alike to engage with the rich tapestry of Catholic art, not as passive observers but as active participants in the unfolding story of salvation. The challenges and opportunities of the modern world call for a renewed creativity, rooted in tradition yet daring to explore new expressions of the eternal truths of our faith.

As we continue to delve into the essence of Catholic creativity, let us remember that our artistic endeavors are part of a greater narrative. They are acts of cooperation with divine grace, seeking to illuminate the path to salvation, educate minds, and convert hearts. In this sacred partnership, artists and their works bear witness to the beauty of the Creator, inviting all to encounter the divine in the midst of the human experience.

From the Catacombs to the Renaissance

In the dimly lit passageways of the early catacombs, where the first Christians sought refuge and solace, one can trace the embryonic stages of Catholic art. These subterranean galleries, adorned with symbols such as the fish (Ichthys), the Good Shepherd, and the orant, encapsulate a profound testimony of faith during a period of persecution. These rudimentary symbols and images, etched and painted upon the walls, served not merely as decorative elements but as potent declarations of the Christian creed and an affirmation of the hope in eternal life. The artistic legacy of Catholicism, hence, roots itself in these catacombs, burgeoning from clandestine tokens of faith to an expansive artistic tradition that heralded the transcendental.

As the peril of persecution waned with the Edict of Milan in 313 AD, the artistic expressions of the Christian faith transitioned from the hiddenness of catacombs to the grandiosity of basilicas. This shift is emblematic of a profound transformation within the Church - from a persecuted sect to an established religion within the Roman Empire. The construction of magnificent basilicas under the patronage of Emperor Constantine and his successors marked a watershed in the history of Catholic art. These edifices served not only as places of worship but also as a testament to the triumph of the Christian faith.

The early medieval period further witnessed the fusion of Christian iconography with the artistic traditions of the Barbarian tribes. The synthesis led to a new vernacular in art, characterized by symbolic motifs and an emphasis on the transcendent. Illuminated manuscripts, such as the Book of Kells, epitomize this era's artistic achievement, weaving intricate designs with Christian symbolism to create a visual gospel that illuminated the minds and hearts towards the divine.

The turn of the first millennium marked the inception of the Romanesque art style, characterized by robust and monumental architecture. This period saw the proliferation of cathedrals and churches across Europe, embodying the Church's growing influence. The Romanesque style, with its rounded arches and massive structures, sought to manifest heaven on earth. The art and architecture of this era encapsulated the majesty and sovereignty of God, drawing the faithful into a sensorial experience of the divine mystery.

The Gothic style emerged from the Romanesque, soaring towards the heavens with its pointed arches, ribbed vaults, and flying buttresses. Cathedrals such as Notre-Dame de Paris and Chartres Cathedral arose as lighthouses of spirituality, their stained-glass windows bathing the interiors in celestial light, narrating biblical stories and theological truths. The Gothic cathedrals were a microcosm of the City of God, bridging the earthy with the heavenly, inviting all into the sacred mystery.

Parallel to the development of monumental architecture was the flowering of theological thought. The scholasticism of the Middle Ages, led by figures like St. Thomas Aquinas, sought to harmonize faith and reason. This intellectual renaissance laid the groundwork for the artistic revival to follow, providing a theological and philosophical underpinning to the aesthetic expressions of the divine. The pursuit of beauty was seen as an encounter with God's own truth, goodness, and beauty.

The devotional life of medieval Christendom also found expression in the burgeoning of religious art. Frescoes, icons, and altarpieces served not only as objects of veneration but as catechetical tools, instructing the faithful in the mysteries of faith. Artists like Giotto and Duccio broke new ground, imbuing their works with emotional depth and a newfound realism, reflecting a deepening personal piety and an intimate encounter with the divine.

The Renaissance, a period of profound cultural and artistic rebirth, marked the culmination of this evolutionary journey of Catholic art. The humanism of the Renaissance did not diminish the religious spirit but rather infused it with a renewed emphasis on the Incarnation's mystery. Artists such as Leonardo da Vinci, Michelangelo, and Raphael, exploring the depths of human experience, created works that were both an homage to God's creation and a mirror of the divine.

The Sistine Chapel, a pinnacle of Renaissance art, serves as a testament to this synthesis of the human and the divine. Michelangelo's ceiling frescoes and his monumental Last Judgment communicate theological truths through the language of beauty and human form, inviting contemplation and conversion.

The transition from the dark corridors of the catacombs to the luminous heights of the Sistine Chapel encapsulates the journey of Catholic art. This evolution, marked by periods of transformation and continuity, mirrors the Church's pilgrimage through history. Catholic art, in its myriad forms across the ages, stands as a testament to the faith's resilience, its capacity for reinvention, and its unending quest for the divine.

The interplay between art and faith throughout this journey underscores the Church's conviction that beauty is a path to God. In every brushstroke, every chiseled stone, and every pane of stained glass lies the human soul's quest for the eternal. Catholic art, from the catacombs to the Renaissance and beyond, thus serves as a bridge between the divine and the human, offering glimpses of heaven amidst the trials and tribulations of earthly life.

In conclusion, the story of Catholic art is not merely a chronicle of aesthetic evolution but a narrative of faith expressed through the tangible and the transcendent. It is a saga of humanity's eternal quest for the divine, a testament to the enduring power of beauty to convey truth, evoke love, and inspire hope.

While this journey from the catacombs to the Renaissance delineates a historical progression, it also symbolizes the perennial nature of Catholic art as a medium of divine revelation and human sanctification. It is, in essence, a pilgrimage of beauty, guiding the soul from the shadows into the light.

Chapter 2: The Role of Talent in Divine Economy

In traversing the landscape of Catholic art and thought, one finds oneself at the juncture where talent not only serves as a conduit for personal expression but also assumes a pivotal role within the divine economy. Talent, seen through the lens of faith, is not a mere accident of birth nor solely a product of human endeavor but a sacred gift bestowed by the Creator for the fulfillment of a higher purpose. This perspective compels us to consider talent as both a divine endowment and a solemn responsibility. By recognizing talent as a gift from God, artists and creators are invited into a participatory role in the ongoing act of creation, called to co-labor with the Divine in the unfolding narrative of salvation and beauty.

The stewardship of talent demands a profound understanding of its purpose beyond personal satisfaction or worldly acclaim. Within the divine economy, talent acts as a leaven, enriching the human community and drawing souls closer to the transcendent reality of God's love. The sanctification of one's gifts through their dedication to God's glory is a form of worship, a sacrifice of praise that transcends the boundaries of the visible world. Here, the artist becomes a mediator, through whom the invisible is made visible, and the divine message of hope, love, and redemption is communicated in a language that transcends words, reaching the depths of the human heart.

Moreover, the proper utilization of talent within the divine economy has a salvific dimension. It is through the beauty and truth conveyed by talent that hearts are stirred, minds are awakened, and souls are moved toward conversion. This transformative power of talent underscores its intrinsic worth and purpose in the divine plan. The role of talent, therefore, extends beyond mere self-expression to become an instrument of education and conversion, enriching the Church and the world with glimpses of the divine splendor. It sets the stage for a dialogue between the Creator and his creation, inviting all to partake in the divine mystery through the sanctification of their gifts.

Talent as a Gift and Responsibility

In the divine economy of creation, each talent bestowed upon humanity is not merely an endowment for personal glory but a sacred trust, imbued with divine intention. This perspective transforms our understanding of talent from a mere ability or skill into a profound gift that carries with it a weight of responsibility. It is through this lens that we begin to explore the purpose and use of talent within the broader context of Catholic art and culture.

At the heart of Catholic teaching is the notion that every gift from God is entrusted to us for the purpose of serving the common good (Catechism of the Catholic Church, 1993). Talent, therefore, is not an isolated or self-serving attribute but one that is inherently social and relational. It is meant to be cultivated, nurtured, and ultimately shared, shining light upon both the creator and the divine inspiration behind the creation.

The parable of the talents, as recounted in the Gospel of Matthew (25:14-30), reinforces the concept of talent as a divine trust. Here, the master entrusts his property to his servants according to their abilities, expecting them to invest and multiply their talents. Upon his return, it is the servant who has buried his talent, failing to multiply it, who is rebuked. This parable serves as a cautionary tale, reminding us that it is through the active engagement and deployment of our talents that we fulfill our part in God's creative work, rather than through their concealment or neglect.

To view talent as a responsibility means recognizing that our creative abilities are a fundamental part of our vocation. In the Catholic tradition, vocation is understood as a calling from God, encompassing not only our professions but our actions, choices, and the overall trajectory of our lives. Talents are entrusted to us within this vocational framework to build up the kingdom of God, to contribute to the church's mission, and to bear witness to the divine amidst the secular.

Art, in its myriad forms, becomes a primary avenue through which talent is realized as a gift and a responsibility. Catholic artists are called to a vocation that transcends mere aesthetic endeavor, becoming co-creators with God in the unfolding narrative of creation. Through their works, artists have the capability to evoke a sense of the transcendent, to uplift the human spirit, and to illuminate truth.

However, this divine partnership also necessitates discernment. The Catholic artist must navigate the waters between the sacred and the secular, ensuring that their talents are not squandered in pursuits that diverge from their divine purpose. It is a delicate balance, demanding a steadfastness in faith and a commitment to the cultivation of talent that is aligned with the teachings of the Church.

The responsibility attached to talent also extends to the mentorship and nurturing of others' talents. Recognizing that the growth of talent within the community represents the flourishing of God's creative gifts, experienced artists are called to mentor emerging talent, guiding them towards a fruitful realization of their gifts. This cyclical process ensures that the divine economy of talent is ever-renewing, reflective of the generative nature of God's creative act.

In conclusion, talent, when viewed through the prism of Catholic thought, is both a gift and a weighty responsibility. It is a means through which the divine becomes manifest in the world, and through which individuals participate in the creative life of God. The cultivation, development, and sharing of talent thus become acts of worship, a response to the call to live out our vocations for the greater glory of God.

As artists and stewards of God's gifts, the challenge is perennial: to use our talents wisely, to bear fruit, and to render, in all our creative endeavors, a portion of the beauty and truth that originate from the Divine Artist Himself.

Utilizing Talent for God's Glory As we segue from the theological underpinnings and the historical journey of Catholic creativity, we arrive at a crucial juncture that bridges the divine gift of talent with its purposeful deployment for glorifying the Creator. The talent bestowed upon individuals is not a mere accident of birth or a personal asset to be exploited for earthly gains. Rather, it is a sacred trust, a veritable shard of the divine light, meant to illuminate the path for others toward the divine.

In the economy of salvation, every talent, be it in the realm of visual arts, music, literature, or any other form of creative expression, holds the potential to be a conduit of grace. When artists embark on the journey of dedicating their talents to God's glory, they partake in a divine collaboration. This process transfigures their work from mere craftsmanship into a liturgy, a worship through the act of creation.

The significance of deploying talent for the glorification of God cannot be overstated. In the Biblical parable of the talents (Matthew 25:14-30), the servants are entrusted with talents, which they are expected to invest wisely. This parable encapsulates the essence of stewardship of talents. Just as the servants are accountable to the master for the use of their talents, so too are artists called to account for how they employ their gifts in the service of the higher good.

Art, in its quintessence, is a reflection of God's creativity, a testament to the infinite beauty and complexity of the Creator. When artists create, they echo the divine act of creation, participating in the unfolding of beauty that draws both creator and beholder closer to the divine mystery. Thus, the work of artists is inherently spiritual, a form of prayer and meditation that spans the bridge between the temporal and the eternal.

Furthermore, talent utilized in the service of God's glory serves as a powerful medium for evangelization. Throughout history, the Church has harnessed the arts as a tool for education, conversion, and the deepening of faith. From the magnificent frescoes of the Sistine Chapel to the sublime compositions of Gregorian chant, art has been a language that transcends words, communicating the truths of the faith to hearts and minds open to the whisperings of the Holy Spirit.

However, the path of dedicating one's talent to God's glory is not devoid of challenges. The secular world often measures success in terms of fame and fortune, metrics that can lure even the most devout artist away from their sacred calling. The struggle between worldly recognition and spiritual fulfillment is a crucible in which the artist's commitment to their divine vocation is tested and refined.

In this journey, the community of faith plays an indispensable role. It provides the support, encouragement, and discernment necessary for artists to navigate the temptations of worldly acclaim. Just as the early Christians supported one another in faith, so too must the contemporary Church be a haven for artists, enabling them to pursue their vocation with conviction and clarity.

To this end, education and formation in the understanding of art's sacred purpose are vital. Artists must be nurtured not only in the development of their technical skills but also in the spiritual depth of their work. They must be taught to see their art not merely as personal expression but as a vocation that demands fidelity to the truth, beauty, and goodness that reflect God's glory.

The fruits of such endeavors are manifold. When talent is harnessed for God's glory, it results in works that possess a transcendent quality, capable of touching the divine. Such works become a beacon of light in a world often shrouded in darkness, drawing all those who encounter them closer to the source of all beauty and truth.

In the final analysis, the utilization of talent for God's glory is a testament to the hope that resides within the human spirit. It is an affirmation of the belief that through our creative endeavors, we can mirror the divine, bringing a foretaste of the heavenly kingdom to earth. This sacred duty, entrusted to artists, is a call to elevate the human experience, to transform the ordinary into the extraordinary, and to lead souls to the ultimate end of their journey – union with God.

As artists navigate the complexities of expressing their faith through their work, they serve as beacons of God's light. In doing so, they not only glorify God but also partake in the divine creativity, weaving threads of the eternal into the tapestry of time. This divine partnership between the Creator and the created elevates the act of creation to a form of worship, a sublime echo of the Creator's voice in the void, calling forth beauty from chaos.

In contemplation of the divine mandate to utilize talent for God's glory, artists are invited to explore the depths of their soul, to discover the unique gifts they have been endowed with, and to commit themselves wholeheartedly to the service of the Greater Good. Through prayer, reflection, and the sacramental life, they can attune their hearts to the whispers of the Holy Spirit, guiding their hands as they create.

Let us then, as a community of believers, support our artists, encouraging them to pursue their heavenly vocation with courage and perseverance. For in their dedication to utilizing talent for God's glory, they become instruments of His peace, architects of beauty, and heralds of the Gospel, bearing witness to the splendor of the Creator, to the ends of the earth.

Chapter 3: Time: The Canvas of Divine Artistry

In the unfolding narrative of salvation, time is not merely a sequential order of events; it is the canvas upon which God displays His divine artistry. The Church, in her wisdom, sanctifies time through the liturgical calendar, imbuing it with a rhythm that mirrors the life of Christ and the history of salvation. This sacred cadence provides a framework for creativity, enabling artists within the Catholic tradition to explore the mysteries of faith across the ages.

At its core, the consecration of time invites us to consider the deeper reality that underpins our existence. The liturgical year, with its seasons of Advent, Christmas, Lent, Easter, and Ordinary Time, functions not as a mere repetition of rituals, but as an ever-deepening spiral into the heart of the divine mystery. Each season offers a unique lens through which the artist can contemplate and express the facets of God's redemptive work in the world.

Advent, characterized by a spirit of expectation and preparation, beckons the artist to dwell on themes of anticipation and hope. It is a time ripe for exploring the virtue of patience and the promise of light breaking into darkness. Christmas, on the other hand, celebrates the Incarnation, God's profound act of entering into human history. This mystery offers rich material for artistic reflection on themes of vulnerability, joy, and divine love manifesting in the humblest of circumstances.

Lent invites a turn inward, a season of penitence and reflection on the reality of sin and the cost of redemption. Artists find in Lent a challenging yet fertile ground for probing the depths of human brokenness and the transformative power of grace. Easter, the pinnacle of the liturgical year, bursts forth as a triumphant affirmation of life over death, light over darkness. It calls artists to bear witness to the joy of the Resurrection and the hope of eternal life through their work.

Ordinary Time, covering the majority of the liturgical calendar, is far from mundane. It is a period of growth, a time for the faithful, including artists, to mature in their spiritual journey and to integrate the mysteries celebrated in the other seasons into daily life. It presents an opportunity to explore the breadth of human experience in light of the Gospel, from the mundane to the extraordinary.

The liturgical calendar, therefore, is not a static entity but a dynamic invitation to view time as a medium through which divine truths are revealed. Just as a painter uses canvas and pigments to bring their vision to life, so does God use time to unfold His divine plan for humanity. Artists, in cooperation with this divine artistry, are called to discern and interpret the signs of the times through their creative endeavors.

This sacred rhythm also confronts the modern tendency to view time as a mere commodity, challenging both artists and the faithful to reclaim it as a gift imbued with eternal significance. In doing so, the artist becomes a prophet, one who sees beyond the temporal to touch the eternal, and through their works, invites others to do the same.

The integrated vision of time offered by the liturgical calendar enriches not only the artist but also the wider community of faith. By engaging with these sacred rhythms, the artist contributes to the evangelizing mission of the Church, proclaiming the Gospel anew for each generation. Their work becomes a bridge between the temporal and the eternal, drawing the beholder into a deeper communion with the divine.

In conclusion, time, as understood and sanctified by the Catholic tradition, provides a rich tapestry for artists to explore the eternal truths of the faith. It is in the interplay of light and darkness, of feasting and fasting, of celebration and contemplation, that the artist finds the raw materials for their creative expression. The liturgical year, with its rhythms and rituals, becomes a source of inspiration and a means of grace, through which the artist participates in God's ongoing act of creation and redemption.

The Sacredness of Time

In understanding the canvas of divine artistry, one must first reckon with the concept of time not merely as a linear progression but as a sacred continuum, imbued with divine significance. The canvas of existence extends beyond the visible, touching the very essence of eternity. This understanding forms the crux of Catholic artistry, where time itself becomes a medium through which divine mysteries are explored and expressed. As such, the Church, in her wisdom, has consecrated the temporal realm through the liturgical calendar, transforming time from mere chronology into a sacred narrative that mirrors the salvific events of Christ's life, death, and resurrection.

Central to this sacred narrative is the cyclical nature of liturgical time, which serves not only to commemorate but to reorient the faithful's journey towards the divine. It's in this cyclical progression that we find a profound reflection of divine artistry, where each season, each feast, each solemnity becomes a brushstroke on the vast canvas of salvation history. This sacred rhythm of time encourages the faithful to contemplate and internalize the mysteries of faith, allowing the external progression of liturgical seasons to mirror the internal spiritual journey towards sanctification.

Furthermore, the sacraments, as outward signs instituted by Christ to confer grace, are deeply intertwined with the concept of sacred time. Each sacramental celebration is a temporal event that transcends time, connecting the participant with the eternal. This sacramental economy showcases the Catholic understanding of time as both a gift and a task—a gift of God's grace that invites cooperation with the divine will and a task that entails the creative unfolding of this grace in the world. In this light, artists and creators possess the unique vocation of making visible the invisible, of rendering temporal the eternal truths of the faith through the tangible medium of their art.

Moreover, the notion of kairos, or God's time, further delineates the sacredness attributed to time in Catholic thought and art. Unlike the chronological time (chronos), kairos signifies the opportune moment—the time of fulfillment and grace. It encapsulates the idea that there are moments when the divine pierces through the fabric of everyday life, revealing that all time is, inherently, God's time. Artists, in their vocation, are called to discern and capture these kairotic moments, to bear witness to the instances when heaven touches earth, and to communicate these glimpses of eternity to a world bound by time.

Thus, the sacredness of time in Catholic artistry serves not only as a theological concept but as a living reality that shapes the creative process. It challenges artists to see beyond the temporal, to imagine and create works that echo the eternal, and to participate in the unfolding of divine beauty within the framework of time. In doing so, they align their creative endeavors with the divine artistry of

God, whose masterful hand weaves the tapestry of time with threads of grace, inviting humanity into the grand narrative of salvation.

Liturgical Time as a Framework for Creativity In the tapestry of Catholic thought and culture, liturgical time stands as a vibrant thread, weaving through the essence of creativity and artistic expression. As the faithful journey through the liturgical year, from the expectant waiting of Advent to the explosive joy of Easter, the rhythmic progression provides not only a spiritual framework but also a canvas for deep creative engagement.

The church, in her wisdom, has delineated time not merely as chronological but as imbued with the sacred. This conception of time as holy invites artists to step into a collaboration with the divine, crafting works that reflect the unfolding mystery of God's plan for humanity. Artists become co-creators, their talents a gift to be used in the service of illustrating and illuminating the faith.

The liturgical calendar with its seasons acts as a guide for the Catholic artist. Advent's themes of anticipation and hope can inspire works that speak to the human condition of waiting and longing. The vibrant hues and imagery associated with Christmas provide a palette for artists to depict the Incarnation, God's ultimate gift of self. In this way, liturgical time challenges the artist to delve deeper, to find those universal human experiences that resonate across time and culture.

Lent, with its emphasis on penance, reflection, and renewal, beckons artists to explore themes of sacrifice, forgiveness, and redemption. The starkness of Good Friday and the glory of Easter Sunday offer stark, powerful contrasts - death and life, despair and hope. Through these, artists can engage with the deepest mysteries of faith, creating works that invite contemplation and conversion.

Ordinary Time, though seemingly less dramatic, is rich with potential for creativity. It represents the lived experience of faith, the day-to-day journey with Christ. This period offers artists the chance to explore the subtleties of spiritual growth and the nuances of God's presence in the mundane.

The liturgical calendar is populated with saints' feast days, each a story of faith lived to the fullest, a potential source of inspiration. Artists might see in these lives a mirror of their own spiritual journey, opportunities to depict the universal call to holiness in diverse and relatable ways.

Moreover, the liturgical cycle with its recurring themes provides a rhythm that can influence the process of creation itself. Artists can find comfort in this rhythm, a structure within which to explore new ideas and revisit old themes. It encourages a discipline of creativity, a commitment to returning to the easel or the keyboard, even when inspiration seems elusive.

This sacred framework fosters an environment where art is not just for art's sake but becomes a vehicle for spiritual enlightenment and nourishment. In aligning their creative endeavors with the liturgical year, artists participate in the evangelizing mission of the Church.

They translate the timeless truths of faith into languages and forms accessible to the contemporary audience.

It's within liturgical time that Catholic art finds its most profound expression. Sacred art created in this context doesn't just decorate or entertain; it serves to elevate the mind and heart to God. It becomes a form of prayer, a meditation that draws both the creator and the viewer deeper into the mystery of faith.

Furthermore, liturgical time challenges Catholic artists to see beauty in transformation and impermanence. Just as the liturgical seasons progress and change, so too does the artist's understanding and expression of truth and beauty. This dynamism can infuse their work with a freshness and vibrancy that speaks to the eternal newness of God's creation.

In essence, the liturgical calendar is not a constraint but a liberation for the Catholic artist. It provides a broad and rich palette of themes, colors, and stories from which to draw. It situates the creative act within the larger story of salvation history, highlighting the transcendent purpose behind the artist's work.

To live and create within this framework is to acknowledge and celebrate the source of all creativity - God the Creator. Artists, in their own way, participate in the divine act of creation, echoing God's love and beauty back into the world. In this sacred partnership, their work becomes more than just personal expression;

it becomes a testament to faith, a beacon of hope, and a source of inspiration for the faithful.

Ultimately, engaging with liturgical time invites Catholic artists to a deeper encounter with the mystery of God, where creativity is not only inspired but sanctified. In this sacred space, artists are called not just to create but to incarnate beauty, truth, and goodness in the world, contributing to the sanctification of time itself.

Thus, the framework of liturgical time is both a challenge and a charism for the Catholic artist. It invites a journey into the heart of faith, where the act of creation becomes a form of worship, a hymn of praise to the Creator who inspires all beauty and imbues every moment with the potential for grace.

Chapter 4: The Symphony of Catholic Art

In the vast expanse of creative endeavors, Catholic art stands as a towering testament to humanity's quest to mirror the divine. Here, within the sacred symbiosis of color, form, and sound, lies a symphony that speaks directly to the soul, transcending time and touching the eternal. This chapter delves into the rich tapestry of visual and musical arts that have been consecrated in the Catholic tradition, revealing how they act as windows to the divine and echoes of heaven, respectively.

The visual arts in Catholicism—encompassing sculpture, painting, and beyond—serve as a vital conduit for spiritual contemplation and worship. Each brushstroke and chisel mark is an act of devotion, a tangible manifestation of the unseen. Through the interplay of light and shadow, artists like Michelangelo and Raphael have not merely depicted biblical narratives but have invited the viewer into a participatory experience of the divine mystery. Their works, alongside countless unnamed artisans who adorned cathedrals and chapels, contribute to a visual symphony that elevates the mind and heart to God.

Parallel to this visual splendor is the celestial harmony of Catholic music. Gregorian chant, with its ethereal melodies, emerges not just as music but as a form of prayer, guiding the faithful towards contemplation and union with the divine. The evolution of sacred music, embracing polyphony and beyond, mirrors the church's journey through history, adapting and evolving, yet always aiming to glorify God and sanctify the faithful.

This synergy between the visual arts and music in Catholicism does more than beautify churches and liturgies; it embodies the church's mission to evangelize. Art and music become languages that can communicate the Gospel across cultural and linguistic barriers, touching hearts and minds in ways words alone cannot. They are not mere embellishments but are integrated into the very life of the Church, enriching its liturgical, pastoral, and educational missions.

Moreover, Catholic art and music encapsulate the concept of 'sacramentality'—that the material world can convey the divine. They act as viaducts through which the sacred breaks into the profane, making the invisible God perceptible to the senses. In this light, artists and musicians engage in a sacred vocation, co-operators with divine grace, tasked with revealing God's presence in the world.

But this divine calling also bears the weight of responsibility. Artists and musicians within the Catholic tradition are stewards of beauty, called to create works that uplift the soul rather than lead it astray. This balance between artistic freedom and moral responsibility has shaped the evolution of Catholic art, ensuring that it remains a source of inspiration, education, and conversion, true to its transcendent purpose.

It's essential to understand that Catholic art is not monolithic; it is as diverse as the universal Church itself. From the ethereal icons of the East to the vibrant tapestries of Latin America, Catholic art reflects the multifaceted face of Christianity. This diversity enriches the symphony of Catholic art, allowing it to speak universally to the human condition while respecting local expressions of faith.

Yet, this symphony faces the challenges of modernity. In an age often characterized by secularism and materialism, Catholic art and music must navigate the tensions between tradition and innovation, sacred and profane. The call to evangelize through beauty requires not just preservation of the past but also engagement with the contemporary world, discerning how to communicate eternal truths to a changing society.

In conclusion, the symphony of Catholic art—its visual and musical expressions—serves as a beacon of divine beauty in a world that yearns for transcendence. As we immerse ourselves in this symphony, let us recognize it as an invitation to encounter God, an act of worship that transcends mere aesthetics, and a call to participate in the unfolding story of salvation. In the echoing chants and the vibrant canvases of Catholic art, we find a reflection of the divine, calling us ever closer to the Creator.

The Visual Arts: A Window to the Divine

In the realm of Catholic tradition, the visual arts serve not merely as aesthetic ventures but as profound vehicles of theological truth, bearing the capacity to reveal the invisible realities of the Divine amidst the tangible. This intrinsic connection between art and faith, where beauty becomes a bridge to the infinite, is a testament to the Church's understanding that every brushstroke, every chisel mark, is an act of worship—a prayer made visible. It is in this sacred dialogue, this synergy of creator and Creator, that art transcends its material bounds to touch the divine.

Historically, the Church has recognized the power of art to communicate complex theological ideas and elevate the mind to contemplation. From the intricate mosaics of early Christian basilicas to the majestic frescoes that adorn the vaults of Renaissance chapels, visual art in its myriad forms has been employed to tell the story of the faith, to educate and to inspire. As St. John Paul II noted, artists, in their creative process, participate in the divine act of creation, echoing God's generative power (John Paul II, 1999). Through their talents, artists offer the world glimpses of the sublime, making the invisible God visible to a world hungry for beauty and truth.

However, the sacred duty of the artist goes beyond mere representation. In the Catholic understanding, art has a redemptive quality, serving as a conduit of grace. By engaging with beauty, the believer is invited into a deeper communion with God, a moment of transcendence where heaven and earth meet. The visual arts, in this light, become a sacramental encounter, a window to the divine, where every color, line, and form speaks of the grandeur of God. It is not just the subject matter—be it the Crucifixion, the Madonna, or the saints—that conveys holiness; it is the very act of artistic creation that sanctifies, transforming the mundane into the extraordinary.

Furthermore, the universal language of art transcends cultural and temporal boundaries, allowing for a unique form of evangelization. In a world where words often fall short, the visual arts communicate the timeless truths of the Catholic faith across ages and to all peoples, irrespective of language or literacy. Indeed, as the Second Vatican Council proclaimed, the Church treasures art as a means to reach the very depths of the human heart, a tool of spiritual awakening and transformation (Second Vatican Council, 1964).

In conclusion, the role of visual arts within Catholicism cannot be overstated; it is at once an homage and a homily, an exploration of divine mystery through the lens of human creativity. As faithful stewards of God's gift, artists are called to a high vocation, crafting works that not only delight the senses but also bring souls closer to the beatific vision. Through the visual arts, the Church continues to affirm that beauty is a vital pathway to God, inviting all to gaze through the window to the divine, where the light of faith illuminates the darkness, guiding the wayward home.

Sculpture and Painting as Acts of Worship In elucidating the essence of Catholic artistic expression, it's paramount to converge upon sculpture and painting not merely as mediums of aesthetic contemplation but as profound acts of worship. The Catholic tradition perceives both sculpture and painting as conduits of divine grace, where the artist, through cooperation with God's creative will, becomes an instrument of the sacred.

The genesis of utilizing art as worship lies deeply interwoven with the Church's history. From the frescoes in the catacombs, where early Christians clandestinely celebrated their faith, to the grandiose altarpieces of the Renaissance, every brushstroke and chisel mark has been infused with a spirit of adoration and divine love. Art, in this theological perspective, transcends human craftsmanship to become a divine act—a prayer embedded in pigment and stone.

Consider, for example, the profound spiritual process behind the creation of a religious painting. The artist engages in a form of prayerful meditation, contemplating the mysteries of faith, before translating these divine revelations onto the canvas. This process is not solely an act of personal faith but serves as a didactic tool, educating the faithful and guiding them towards a deeper communion with the divine.

Sculpture, with its tangible, three-dimensional presence, offers another unique pathway to divine encounter. The great cathedrals of Europe, adorned with statues of saints and Biblical narratives carved in stone, stand testament to sculpture's potential to manifest the holy amidst the mundane. These sacred figures, occupying physical space alongside the worshipper, act as mediators—bridging the chasm between the celestial and the terrestrial.

Significantly, the Church has long recognized the sacrosanct nature of such artistic endeavors. Sacred art is encased within a framework of liturgical and canonical guidelines designed to preserve the integrity of its worshipful purpose. This is not to constrain creativity but to ensure that every stroke and sculpt bears right witness to the truths of the Catholic faith. To this end, the Church affirms that genuine religious art is an effective means of opening the human heart to the realities of Heaven (Vatican II, 1963).

Yet, the act of creation is also an act of personal sanctification for the artist. In aligning their talent with God's creative power, artists partake in a deeply transformative process. They journey from mere creators of beauty to co-creators with the Divine, their work sanctifying not just the space it occupies but their very being.

This vocation of artists to serve as conduits of the sacred is magnificently encapsulated in the life and works of countless Catholic artists throughout history. From the ethereal mosaics of Ravenna to Michelangelo's resplendent Sistine Chapel ceiling, these works are not just art; they are visual hymns of praise and supplication to the Almighty.

In modern times, the call to create as an act of worship remains undiminished. Despite the secular pressures and myriad interpretations of art in the contemporary era, the creation of sacred art endures as a potent means of evangelization and catechesis. Today's Catholic artists, sculptors, and painters continue to embed the gospel message within their works, offering new generations a visual lexicon of faith.

The pedagogical value of sacred art cannot be overstated. Through the depiction of biblical stories, saints' lives, and doctrinal truths, art serves as a catechetical tool, rendering the sublime teachings of the Church accessible and comprehensible to all, irrespective of their level of education or literacy. This democratization of faith through art has been a cornerstone of Catholic evangelization, allowing the Church to reach souls across cultural and temporal divides.

Yet, the creation of sacred art also poses unique challenges in the modern age, from the commercialization of religious images to the erosion of traditional skills. Navigating these trials requires a re-affirmation of art's intrinsic worshipful purpose—a recognition that every creative act is a reflection of the Creator himself.

The education of future generations of Catholic artists is, therefore, of paramount importance. By fostering an environment where young talents are nurtured within the bosom of the Church, we ensure the continuity of this rich legacy of sacred art as an act of worship. Institutions, parishes, and individuals must collaborate to support the flourishing of Catholic arts, recognizing their role in the divine economy of salvation.

In conclusion, the vocation of the Catholic artist is a noble and holy calling, an invitation to participate in the ongoing narrative of salvation through the medium of beauty. Sculpture and painting, when approached as acts of worship, have the power to transform hearts, minds, and souls, drawing all closer to the ineffable mystery of God's love.

Let us, therefore, cherish and support the sacred arts, nurturing the talents entrusted to our care, that through our collective creativity, the Church may continue to be a beacon of divine beauty in the world—a mirror reflecting the glory of Heaven itself.

Music: Echoes of Heaven

The journey through Catholic art has unfolded a tapestry rich in color and form, leading us now to the ethereal realm of Music, where sound becomes an echo of the divine. In the symphony of Catholic art, music holds a distinct place, for it is with music that the invisible is rendered audible, transcending the limitations of human expression to unveil a glimpse of the heavenly.

In the realm of sacred music, one finds the unique capacity for the human soul to encounter the divine. This encounter is not merely an intellectual exercise but an experiential communion with the Divine through the beauty and harmony of sound. Catholic music, in its purest form, evokes the ineffable mystery of God, inviting the faithful into a deeper relationship with their Creator. It serves not only as an act of worship but as a catalyst for spiritual transformation, aiding the faithful in their quest for sanctity and communion with the divine.

Throughout history, the Church has recognized the profound impact of music on worship and the spiritual life. From the earliest chants of the Christian tradition to the complex polyphony of the Renaissance, music has been woven into the fabric of Catholic worship, reflecting the evolving tapestry of faith across centuries. The development of Gregorian chant, a hallmark of Western sacred music, epitomizes this integration of art and faith, where melody becomes prayer, elevating the mind and heart to God (Hiley, 1993).

Yet, the significance of music extends beyond its liturgical function. It embodies the Catholic imagination, harnessing human creativity and talent as a reflection of the Divine Creator. In the intricate compositions of sacred music, one discerns a microcosm of divine order—a harmony that mirrors the cosmic balance instilled by God. This celestial harmony, achieved through the disciplined mastery of musical form, acts as a conduit of grace, elevating the human spirit towards the transcendent.

Moreover, Catholic music serves as an instrument of evangelization, transcending linguistic and cultural barriers to touch the hearts of believers and seekers alike. The universality of music makes it a powerful medium for conveying the truths of the faith, capable of inspiring conversion and renewing the Church. In the echoes of sacred music, one finds an invitation to explore the depths of Catholic tradition, heritage, and the profound mysteries of faith.

In contemporary times, the challenge lies in preserving the sacredness of music amidst a culture often dominated by secular influences. The Church must navigate the delicate balance between tradition and innovation, ensuring that music remains a genuine expression of worship and a means of encountering God. Composers of faith today are called to draw inspiration from the rich heritage of sacred music while exploring new expressions of the divine in sound, striving to create works that resonate with the modern soul yet are anchored in timeless truth.

The vitality of music in Catholic worship and its role in the spiritual life cannot be overstated. As St. Augustine famously remarked, "He who sings prays twice." This duality of music as both art and prayer encapsulates its profound significance in the Catholic tradition. It uplifts the soul, fortifies the faith, and glorifies God, serving as a foretaste of the heavenly liturgy that awaits the faithful.

As we delve into the intricacies of Catholic music, from Gregorian chant to contemporary compositions, we embark on a journey that transcends time and space. We discover in music an echo of heaven—a harmonious reflection of the divine that leads the soul closer to the eternal. In this symphony of Catholic art, music stands as a testament to the beauty of divine creation, inviting us to partake in the celestial chorus that praises God for eternity.

In the grand design of the Catholic artistic tradition, music plays an indispensable role, weaving together the threads of heaven and earth. It beckons us to listen with the ears of the heart, to perceive the divine melodies that permeate our world, and to allow the echoes of heaven to transform our lives. In the sacred sounds of Catholic music, we find a powerful expression of faith, a beacon of hope, and a source of inspiration on our journey towards the Divine.

Gregorian Chant and Beyond Within the hallowed halls of
Catholic tradition, music has perennially soared as a bridge between
the divine and the ephemeral, connecting the human spirit directly to
the heavens. The genesis of this sacred symphony within the
Church's liturgical life is intrinsically tied to Gregorian chant,
named after Pope Gregory I, who, while not the founder, was a
pivotal figure in its promotion and organization during the late 6th
and early 7th centuries. This melodic prayer is not merely an art
form but an audible manifestation of faith, a direct communication
with the Divine that transcends mere words.

The chant's pure, unadorned melody, sung in Latin, encapsulates the
profound simplicity of spiritual pursuit, stripping away the
complexities of language and cultural barriers to speak directly to
the soul. Interestingly, the structure of Gregorian chant—free from
meter and accompanied only by the natural rhythm of the text—
mirrors the eternal flow of time in the presence of the Infinite,
inviting the faithful into a timeless communion with God.

It would be remiss, however, to perceive Gregorian chant as an
isolated phenomenon within the extensive panorama of Catholic
musical tradition. Rather, it serves as the foundational bedrock upon
which the edifice of sacred music has been built. Over the centuries,
the evolution of this music has seen the incorporation of polyphony,
where the intertwining of multiple independent melodic lines

created a complex, harmonious tapestry reflecting the intricate nature of divine truth.

Composers such as Palestrina in the Renaissance period became architects of the celestial, their compositions embodying an ethereal beauty that elevates the spirit. Palestrina's work, grounded in the principles of chant, evolved into a form that respected the clarity of the liturgical text while introducing a richer harmonic landscape, an allegory of the multifaceted ways in which the divine can be encountered.

As history unfurled, the Baroque era witnessed the sacred merge with the dramatic, encapsulated most notably in the works of Bach. His compositions, though more elaborate, remained deeply spiritual, a testament to the power of music to convey theological truths and invoke deep religious experience.

The journey of sacred music through the ages mirrors the Church's ongoing pilgrimage through time—adapting, evolving, but always with the aim of drawing souls closer to the Divine. As the Gregorian chant laid the foundation, subsequent forms of sacred music built upon it, each generation finding new expressions of age-old truths, ensuring that the faith remains ever alive, ever relevant.

In the contemporary landscape, the spirit of Gregorian chant lives on, not only in its pure form but also as inspiration for modern composers who seek to blend ancient tradition with contemporary sensibilities. The stark, unembellished beauty of the chant continues to find echoes in new compositions that seek to express the timeless in our time.

The transmission of this rich musical heritage continues through the Church's liturgical life, in the monastic communities that still chant the hours, and in parishes and cathedrals around the world where the faithful gather to worship. Within these sacred spaces, Gregorian chant remains a living link to the past, a reminder of the Church's temporal and timeless journey.

Moreover, the study and performance of Gregorian chant and its subsequent musical evolutions serve not only as an exercise in historical preservation but as an act of worship itself. Choirs and scholas dedicate themselves to this art, their voices joining in a centuries-long chorus of praise and prayer that rises to the heavens.

This tradition of sacred music, with Gregorian chant at its heart, exemplifies the Church's understanding of beauty as a path to God. It manifests the belief that through the beautiful—whether in form, harmony, or melody—the divine breaks into the world, offering glimpses of eternity.

Thus, the evolution from Gregorian chant to the rich tapestry of sacred music that followed reflects a deeper theological and philosophical truth: that in every age, humanity seeks to articulate its encounter with the divine through the medium of art. Music, in its most sublime form, becomes a vehicle through which the soul's deepest yearnings for the transcendent are expressed and fulfilled.

In essence, the journey from Gregorian chant and beyond is a testament to the dynamic interplay between tradition and innovation in the realm of Catholic spirituality. It underscores the Church's role as custodian of a sacred tradition that continuously evolves, breathing new life into ancient forms to meet the longing of contemporary hearts for transcendence and communion with the Divine.

It is within this ever-evolving symphony of faith that Gregorian chant maintains its relevance, not as a relic of the past, but as a vibrant and living expression of the Church's eternal mission to elevate the human spirit to the divine. In this light, the journey of sacred music within the Catholic tradition—rooted in the purity of chant and extending into the complexities of modern composition—stands as a profound witness to the enduring power of art to connect humanity with the Divine.

Chapter 5: Catholic Literature: Narratives of Faith

In the grand tapestry of Catholic tradition, literature holds a place of particular reverence, serving not only as a vessel for theological insight and historical record but also as a medium through which the depth and breadth of human experience can be explored and understood. The narratives of faith that unfold within Catholic literature act as both mirror and window: a mirror reflecting our own spiritual journeys, and a window opening onto vistas of divine mystery.

At the heart of this tradition are the lives of the saints, those spiritual giants whose journeys have been recorded and celebrated in texts that span centuries. These stories are not mere biographies; they are spiritual maps, guides that offer insight into the nature of holiness and the path to sanctity. They challenge, inspire, and offer a vision of life transformed by grace. The power of such narratives in evangelization cannot be overstated, as they provide tangible examples of divine virtues in human lives (Wallace, 2015).

Moreover, the very act of storytelling within the Catholic context serves a profound purpose. It is an act of communion, linking the storyteller and listener in a shared experience of the sacred. In this way, Catholic literature participates in the sacramental economy of the Church, where divine truths are made accessible through material realities. This literature, therefore, becomes a conduit of grace, educating and converting not through didactic instruction but through the power of the story itself.

One cannot overlook the allegorical dimension of Catholic literature, where narratives operate on multiple levels of meaning. Much like the parables of Christ, these stories engage not only the mind but also the heart and soul. The allegorical mode invites readers into a deeper engagement with the text, revealing truths that are not immediately obvious and offering multiple layers of interpretation.

In the contemporary world, Catholic literature assumes a renewed importance. In a culture often marked by relativism and a crisis of meaning, narratives of faith stand out as beacons of hope and sources of truth. They offer answers to the ultimate questions about human existence, purpose, and destiny, grounded in a tradition that has wrestled with these questions for millennia.

It's worth considering the creative process behind Catholic literature as a collaboration with divine inspiration. Authors engaged in creating Catholic narratives embark on a journey that is both profoundly personal and deeply communal. They become vessels through which the Holy Spirit can speak, translating the ineffable mysteries of faith into stories and characters that resonate with the human heart.

In conclusion, Catholic literature, with its rich tradition of narratives of faith, functions as a vital medium of evangelization, education, and conversion. Through the power of storytelling, it opens up horizons of understanding, allowing readers to glimpse the beauty and depth of the Catholic faith. It educates the mind, converts the heart, and elevates the soul, exemplifying how human talents, when cooperated with divine grace, can achieve ends that resonate with eternal significance.

The Power of Storytelling in Evangelization

Throughout the annals of history, the Catholic Church has harnessed the profound power of storytelling in the mission of evangelization. It's an incontrovertible fact that narratives—be they lived, written, or visualized—hold a unique capacity to touch the human heart, to transform the mundane into the divine, and to usher the soul into the sacred canopy of faith. In the realm of Catholic literature, this power is not only recognized but revered and leveraged as a pivotal tool in the spiritual journey of both the teller and the listener.

At the heart of Catholic storytelling lies the life of Jesus Christ—the greatest story ever told—a narrative that has been recounted and reflected upon in countless ways through the ages. This foundational story informs and inspires all Catholic narrative, serving as the ultimate exemplar of how stories can change hearts, minds, and, ultimately, lives. From this central narrative emerge the lives of the saints, parables, and allegories, each a testament to the transcendent truth, beauty, and goodness found in the gospels.

In the annals of Catholic literature, saints' lives have served as particularly potent tools for evangelization. These narratives, rich in virtue, sacrifice, and unwavering faith, act as mirrors reflecting the light of Christ to the reader. Saints' biographies illuminate the path for the faithful, showcasing the diverse ways in which God calls each individual to live out their faith in the world. It is through these stories that believers and non-believers alike can glimpse the celestial within the corporeal, the eternal promise within temporal striving.

Moreover, Catholic literature extends its evangelizing mission through allegory and symbolism, inviting deeper contemplation and engagement with the faith. Works like Dante's *Divine Comedy* or the parables told by Jesus himself in the New Testament use the art of storytelling to peel back the layers of human experience, revealing the spiritual realities that underlie our existence. Such narratives invite the reader into a pilgrimage of the mind and soul towards understanding, conversion, and ultimately, communion with the Divine.

The act of storytelling within the Catholic tradition is not merely a transmission of facts or doctrines but is fundamentally incarnational. It mirrors the Incarnation of Christ, making the divine accessible and relatable through the human experience. This incarnational approach underpins the effectiveness of storytelling in evangelization, as it naturally facilitates a connection between the story and the listener's own life, inviting an encounter with God that is deeply personal and transformative.

Evangelization through storytelling is further empowered by its communal aspect. Stories within the Catholic faith are not meant to be hoarded or hidden but shared and spread like the seeds of the sower. When a story resonates with an individual, it becomes a bridge to others, fostering a sense of belonging and community. This communal sharing of stories reaffirms the universal call to holiness and the shared journey of faith, thereby strengthening the Body of Christ.

Furthermore, the adaptability of storytelling allows it to traverse cultures, languages, and epochs, embodying the catholic—that is, universal—nature of the Church. Stories can be reinterpreted and retold in ways that are relevant to different contexts, making the timeless truths of the Catholic faith accessible to all peoples, in all places, at all times. This enduring relevance ensures that Catholic storytelling remains a powerful evangelizing force in the modern world.

In conclusion, the power of storytelling in evangelization is an indispensable treasure of the Catholic Church. It harnesses the innate human love for stories to draw individuals closer to the divine, weaving the thread of faith through the tapestry of human history. As we continue to tell and retell these sacred narratives, we participate in the ongoing story of salvation, inviting all to encounter Christ and His Church.

Saints' Lives as Inspirational Texts Within the rich tapestry of Catholic literature, the lives of the saints hold a special place, serving not only as historical accounts but also as profound sources of inspiration. These stories, steeped in the trials, tribulations, and triumphs of individuals who have navigated the path of faith before us, offer a unique lens through which we can examine our own spiritual journeys. It is in the careful study and contemplation of these narratives that we, as followers of Christ, can find guidance, motivation, and a deeper sense of connection to the divine artistry that shapes our lives.

The impact of the saints' lives on the Catholic imagination cannot be overstated. These narratives provide vivid illustrations of virtue in action, embodying the theological and moral principles that are the bedrock of Catholic teaching. They act as mirrors reflecting the myriad ways in which divine grace manifests in human existence, often in the most unexpected circumstances. As such, they are not merely stories to be read but lived experiences to be emulated, deeply intertwined with the fabric of Catholic culture and spirituality.

In approaching the lives of the saints as inspirational texts, it is essential to recognize their dual nature as both historical documents and allegorical tales designed to impart spiritual wisdom. This duality is a hallmark of the Catholic intellectual tradition, which holds that truth can be conveyed through both literal and symbolic means. The saints' stories encapsulate this principle, providing a bridge between the temporal and the eternal, the mundane and the divine.

Art enthusiasts, Roman Catholics, art professors, and students alike can draw from these stories a wellspring of creative inspiration. For the artist, the saints' lives offer rich material for exploration in visual arts, literature, and music, presenting opportunities to translate spiritual ideals into tangible forms that speak to the heart of human experience. In this way, the act of creating based on the saints' narratives becomes an act of faith, a form of worship that mirrors the divine act of creation itself.

The educational value of the saints' stories is equally profound. For students and professors, these narratives serve as powerful tools for investigating the intersection of faith, culture, and art. They provide a concrete context within which to explore abstract theological concepts, making the teachings of the Church more accessible and relatable. Furthermore, studying these stories in an academic setting encourages critical thinking and fosters a deeper understanding of the cultural and historical forces that have shaped the development of Catholic thought and tradition.

From a spiritual perspective, the lives of the saints are a source of perpetual encouragement, reminding us that holiness is attainable and that the path to sainthood is tread by ordinary people who respond to God's call with extraordinary love and fidelity. These stories demonstrate that every moment of our lives, no matter how mundane or challenging, is charged with the potential for sanctity. They invite us to view our own experiences through the lens of grace, seeking the divine purpose in every joy, sorrow, and trial.

The role of saints' narratives in the process of evangelization cannot be overlooked. In a world hungry for meaning and authenticity, these stories offer compelling evidence of the transformative power of faith. They serve as testimonies to the reality of God's work in the world, drawing people to the Church by illustrating the beauty and richness of the Catholic spiritual tradition. Through their example, the saints become ambassadors of Christ, beckoning others to embark on their own journeys of faith.

Moreover, the saints' lives are a testament to the universal call to holiness, a central theme of the Second Vatican Council. They remind us that sainthood is not reserved for a select few but is attainable for all who seek to live their lives in conformity with God's will. This realization can inspire a renewed sense of purpose and direction, motivating individuals to pursue a deeper engagement with their faith and a more active participation in the life of the Church.

In contemplating the saints' lives, we are also confronted with the reality of suffering and the redemptive value it can hold within the context of faith. Many saints endured profound hardships, yet their stories reveal how suffering, when united with Christ's own suffering, can become a powerful means of spiritual growth and a source of grace for others. This perspective offers a radically countercultural view of suffering, challenging the prevailing attitudes of avoidance and despair.

The saints also serve as models of virtue in a world that often seems to have lost sight of the importance of moral integrity and character. In their stories, we encounter exemplars of courage, humility, charity, patience, and countless other virtues that are desperately needed in contemporary society. By studying their lives, we are encouraged to cultivate these virtues in our own lives, contributing to the renewal of the moral fabric of the world around us.

In conclusion, the lives of the saints, as recounted in inspirational texts, play a crucial role in the life of the Catholic Church and its faithful. They are not simply stories from the past but living narratives that continue to influence and shape the present and future of the Church. As sources of inspiration, education, and spiritual nourishment, they provide a roadmap for navigating the complexities of human existence, pointing us toward the ultimate destination of our journey: union with God.

Chapter 6: The Cathedrals of Thought: Catholic Philosophy and Theology

In the grand tapestry of Catholic tradition, philosophy and theology stand as monolithic cathedrals of thought, realms where the intellectual pursuit of truth engages harmoniously with divine revelation. This chapter ventures into the heart of these magnificent edifices, exploring how Catholic philosophy and theology have shaped not just ecclesiastical discourse but also the broader cultural landscape, particularly in the arts.

The Scholastic heritage, a beacon of this intellectual tradition, represents an era where the greatest minds sought to integrate faith and reason. Scholastics like Thomas Aquinas and Bonaventure did not see faith and reason as opponents but as two wings on which the human spirit rises to the contemplation of truth. Their work provides a foundation for understanding the divine, not as a distant mystery, but as the ultimate reality that can be approached through rigorous intellectual endeavor.

This integration of faith and reason inspired a renaissance in Catholic philosophy and theology, where the pursuit of truth became an act of worship. For these medieval scholars, the exploration of philosophy was not merely an academic exercise but a sacred journey towards God. Their dedication reminds us that the truths we seek in the arts, sciences, and humanities are reflections of the divine truth.

The influence of Catholic theology on the visual arts is profound and undeniable. Cathedrals themselves, with their breathtaking architecture, are embodiments of theological principles, designed to lift the human mind and heart to God. The Gothic cathedrals of medieval Europe, with their upward-sweeping lines and light-filled spaces, are visual sermons on the nature of God's transcendence and immanence.

Moreover, the theological concept of incarnation deeply influenced Christian art, encouraging a portrayal of the divine made flesh. Artists sought to capture the mystery of the Incarnation, leading to a rich tradition of religious art that depicts not just the divinity of Christ but his humanity as well. This approach to art highlights the profound Catholic belief in the sanctity and dignity of the human person, created in the image of God.

In literature, Catholic theology has inspired countless works that explore the depths of human sin and divine redemption. From Dante's "Divine Comedy" to Graham Greene's novels, Catholic writers have used their craft to wrestle with the mysteries of faith, evil, salvation, and grace, creating works of profound beauty and spiritual insight.

Music, too, has been a conduit for theological expression, with composers like Palestrina and Bach creating works that convey the beauty and complexity of the divine. Gregorian chant, in particular, embodies the theological virtue of hope, with its simple melodies evoking a sense of peace and contemplation.

Theological themes of creation, fall, redemption, and eschatology have also enriched the narrative arts, providing a framework for stories that reflect the human condition in light of divine truth. These stories, whether told through stained glass, frescoes, or motion pictures, invite reflection on the eternal questions of love, justice, suffering, and salvation.

Importantly, Catholic theology emphasizes the communal aspect of faith, influencing the development of art forms that foster communal participation and identity. From liturgical music to religious processions, the arts serve not only as expressions of individual faith but as acts of communal worship and memory.

The role of the artist in this theological framework is not merely that of a creator but as a co-creator with God. Catholic theology affirms the dignity of human creativity as a participation in the divine act of creation, challenging artists to see their work as a vocation to reveal God's truth and beauty to the world.

This understanding of art as a vocation is central to the Catholic view of culture. Art, in its highest form, is not simply for art's sake but for the sake of illuminating the divine reality, leading others to encounter God through beauty. In this sense, artists are custodians of the sacred, tasked with opening windows to the divine in the midst of the secular world.

However, this vision of art as a sacramental encounter with the divine calls for a discernment that can navigate the complexities of modern culture while remaining rooted in the eternal truths of the faith. It requires a constant dialogue between the traditions of the past and the innovations of the present, between the truths of revelation and the discoveries of human reason.

In conclusion, Catholic philosophy and theology provide a rich soil from which the arts can flourish, offering insights that elevate the human experience and draw us closer to the divine. The cathedrals of thought erected by Catholic thinkers are not only monuments to intellectual achievement but sanctuaries where the soul can encounter the living God, through the beauty and truth found in the arts.

The Scholastic Heritage

The expanse of Catholic thought, with its deep roots in the scholastic tradition, stands as a monumental testament to the Church's pursuit of understanding the divine through the lens of human reason. At the heart of this pursuit was a remarkable confluence of faith and reason, a symbiotic relationship that has shaped Catholic philosophy and theology through the centuries. This interplay between belief and intellect, often seen as divergent forces in the secular realm, found its most profound expression in the scholasticism of the Middle Ages.

Scholasticism, with its rigorous analytical approach and methodical examination of theological questions, emerged as a beacon of intellectual inquiry. It sought to reconcile the wisdom of ancient philosophers with Christian doctrines, creating a rich tapestry of thought that has influenced not just religious discourse but the foundations of Western philosophy itself. The scholastics, in their timeless quest for knowledge, viewed reason as a gift from God, a tool to explore the mysteries of faith and the natural order.

The medieval universities were the crucibles in which this intellectual alchemy took place. Masters like Albert the Great and his illustrious pupil, Thomas Aquinas, walked their halls, teaching and writing works that would become cornerstones of Catholic thought. Aquinas, in particular, with his "Summa Theologica," epitomized the scholastic method. His efforts to harmonize faith with Aristotelian philosophy underscore the scholastic aim to demonstrate that the truths of faith and the truths of reason are not in conflict but are part of a single truth seen from different perspectives.

It was in these scholastic circles that the notion of theology as the "queen of the sciences" took root. This idea elevated theology to the highest order of scholarly disciplines, asserting that the study of God and divine things offered the ultimate framework within which all other knowledge could be understood. The scholastics argued that since all truth is God's truth, no genuine conflict between faith and reason could exist. Their work laid the groundwork for a perennial philosophy that saw the natural world as a reflection of divine order, intelligible and accessible to human understanding.

However, scholasticism was not a monolith. Within its broad canopy, debates and disagreements flourished. Realism and nominalism, for instance, represented two opposing trends in scholastic thought, each with its views on the nature of universals and their existence outside the human mind. These debates were not mere academic exercises; they reflected deeper questions about God's nature, human knowledge, and the structure of reality itself.

Despite its intellectual rigor and theological depth, scholasticism faced criticism and evolution over time. The Renaissance and the Reformation brought new challenges and shifts in thought, leading to a diversification of scholastic methodology. Yet, the enduring legacy of scholasticism lies in its bold assertion of the compatibility of faith and reason. This legacy is the cornerstone of Catholic intellectual tradition, paving the way for modern Catholic thought to engage with contemporary issues while remaining anchored in its rich scholastic heritage.

In light of this tradition, the Church has continually called for a "new evangelization," one that bridges the ancient with the modern, engaging with the world through the lens of faith informed by reason. The Second Vatican Council, with documents like "Gaudium et Spes," echoed the scholastic heritage in its call for dialogue with the modern world, emphasizing the role of the Church in illuminating the path to truth in an age often marked by skepticism.

The scholastic heritage, then, serves not only as a historical benchmark of Catholic thought but also as a vibrant, living tradition that continues to inform the Church's engagement with the world. In the grand cathedrals of thought that the scholastics built, modern Catholics find both a treasury of wisdom and a compass for navigating the complexities of contemporary life. The scholastic emphasis on the harmony of faith and reason remains a beacon of hope, reassuring the faithful that in the pursuit of truth, they are not wandering in the dark but walking in the light of God's wisdom.

The enduring strength of the scholastic tradition lies in its unyielding commitment to truth, its recognition of the power of human reason sanctified by faith. As the Church faces new challenges and enters into new dialogues, the scholastic heritage reminds us of the richness of Catholic intellectual tradition. It beckons us to continue exploring, questioning, and understanding, always with the assurance that in seeking truth, we draw closer to the divine.

In conclusion, the scholastic heritage is not merely a chapter in the history of Catholic thought but a living stream that feeds the Church's mission in the world today. As artists, theologians, philosophers, and believers, we are heirs to this legacy. It calls us to view our creative and intellectual endeavors as part of a larger, divine tapestry, woven through the ages with the threads of faith and reason. In this context, our work becomes a continuation of the scholastics' sacred quest, a testament to the enduring power of Catholic art and thought to illuminate, inspire, and transform.

Continuing from the previous discussions on the profound role that Catholic art plays in expressing and nurturing faith, it becomes essential to delve into a cornerstone of Catholic intellectual tradition: the integration of faith and reason. This integration is not merely a theological or philosophical stance but a dynamic principle that infuses Catholic creativity, especially within the realms of art and beauty.

Integrating Faith and Reason as it unfolds within the Catholic tradition is akin to the harmonious coalescence of two rivers into a single, mightier force. In the Catholic worldview, faith and reason are not antagonists but companions in the quest to understand and express the divine mystery. This integration underpins the belief that God is the source of all truth, whether revealed through the sacred scriptures or discovered through human intellect and reason. Such a premise posits that truth, in its essence, is unified. Hence, the pursuit of truth, whether through the lens of faith or the rigor of reason, ultimately leads toward the same divine reality.

In the realm of Catholic art, this confluence of faith and reason becomes particularly evident. The creation of art, in this perspective, is not a mere manifestation of individualistic expression or aesthetic pursuit but a deeply theological act. It is where the beauty that draws the mind and heart to wonder and awe is recognized as a reflection of the divine beauty. This theological underpinning of art allows Catholic artists to employ their talent, intellect, and spiritual insight to translate theological truths into visual, literary, or performative mediums.

The symbiotic relationship between faith and reason in Catholic art affords a unique lens through which the divine mysteries are explored and communicated. For instance, the intricate designs of Gothic cathedrals are not merely architectural feats but physical representations of theological concepts, embodying the scholastic belief in an orderly, rational universe created by a divine intelligence. Similarly, the narrative depth of Biblical stories depicted in Renaissance paintings extends an invitation to the viewers to engage both intellectually and spiritually with the scenes portrayed.

This duality of engagement is crucial for the Catholic artist and the beholder of art. The artist, in integrating faith and reason, becomes a mediator between the divine and the human. Through their work, they offer a pathway for the viewer to encounter spiritual truths through the tangible medium of art. This encounter is not passive but engages the viewer in an active process of reflection, challenging them to use both heart and mind to grasp the transcendent truths depicted.

Moreover, the integration of faith and reason within Catholic art serves a pedagogical function. Art becomes a vehicle for expressing complex theological concepts and moral teachings in a manner that is accessible and engaging. In this context, art does not merely inform but also forms its audience, shaping the viewer's understanding of and relationship with the divine.

The challenge for the Catholic artist, therefore, lies in traversing the delicate balance between maintaining theological integrity and exercising creative freedom. This challenge, however, also presents an opportunity for innovation within the tradition. By integrating faith and reason, artists can explore new forms and expressions that resonate with contemporary audiences while remaining rooted in the timeless truths of the Catholic faith.

In conclusion, the integration of faith and reason within Catholic art is a testament to the Church's conviction that the divine can be encountered through the created world. It underscores the role of art as a bridge between the human and the divine, inviting both the creator and the beholder into a deeper engagement with the mystery of existence. Through this integration, Catholic art continues to offer fresh perspectives on the divine, inviting all who encounter it to a journey of faith enlightened by reason.

Chapter 7: Saints: The Masterpieces of God

In the preceding chapters, we have journeyed through the labyrinthine corridors of Catholic creativity, exploring the ways in which art and divinity intertwine to weave a tapestry of faith. Now, we arrive at the heart of this exploration: the saints, those masterpieces crafted by the hand of God Himself. These luminaries of holiness serve as the ultimate confluence of divine talent and human cooperation, embodying the notion that the human soul, touched by grace, can transcend its earthly confines to reflect the beauty of the Creator.

The art of holiness, as exemplified in the lives of the saints, is not merely a pursuit of moral excellence but a profound participation in the divine mystery. Each saint, in their unique way, becomes a canvas on which God's grace is vividly depicted. The saints' lives, with their dramatic contours of struggle, conversion, and sanctity, offer a rich source of inspiration not only for believers but for anyone who appreciates the profound capacity of the human spirit to transcend its limitations.

Among these celestial masterpieces, certain saints stand out as patrons of the arts, embodying the intrinsic connection between creating art and manifesting holiness. Saint Catherine of Bologna, for instance, is venerated as the patron saint of artists. Her treatise, "The Seven Spiritual Weapons Necessary for Spiritual Warfare," though primarily a spiritual guide, also reflects her deep artistic sensibility, having been a skilled painter in her lifetime. Saints like Catherine remind us that the act of creating, whether it be a painting, a sculpture, or a literary work, is inherently imbued with the potential for sanctity.

The relationship between saints and art is symbiotic. While the saints inspire art, art, in turn, immortalizes saints, capturing their essence and continuing their legacy through time. The veneration of saints through art serves not only as a means of education and inspiration but also as an act of devotion itself. Through the ages, artists have strived to encapsulate the holy ecstasy of Saint Teresa of Avila, the profound humility of Saint Francis of Assisi, and the burning charity of Saint Vincent de Paul, thereby transmitting the spiritual charisma of the saints to the wider community of believers and beyond.

This transmission of sanctity through art possesses a transformative power, for both the creator and the observer. In the act of depicting the saints, artists themselves embark on a spiritual odyssey, engaging in a dialogue with the divine that transcends mere representation. Observers, on the other hand, are drawn into the narrative of holiness, invited to reflect on their own spiritual journey and potential for sanctity.

The saints exert a profound influence on Catholic thought and culture, serving as exemplars of the integration of faith and reason, creativity and dogma. Their lives affirm the belief that the divine infiltrates every aspect of human existence and that every act of creation is a potential act of sanctity. As such, the saints inspire not only artists but all who seek to live a life of purpose and grace.

In contemplating the saints as "The Masterpieces of God," we are reminded of our own call to holiness. Each individual, in their unique existence, has the capacity to become a vessel of divine beauty. The lives of the saints challenge us to view our own experiences through the lens of potential sanctity, recognizing that every moment holds the possibility for grace.

Thus, the narrative of the saints is not merely a history to be revered but a living testament to the transformative power of faith and creativity. They stand as beacons of hope and beauty, guiding humanity towards its ultimate purpose: union with the divine,".

In conclusion, the saints, as God's masterpieces, illuminate the path towards the divine, showcasing the prolific intersection between art and sanctity. Their lives, immortalized through art and veneration, continue to inspire, educate, and challenge us, serving as eternal witnesses to the omnipresence of God's grace in the world.

The Art of Holiness

In the tapestry of Catholic tradition, the saints hold a special place as luminaries guiding the faithful toward higher virtues and closer communion with the divine. Just as art captures the ineffable beauty of the world and transcends the mundane, the lives of saints serve as masterpieces of God's grace, imbuing the spiritual landscape with color, depth, and inspiration. This section explores the intersection of sanctity and creativity, unveiling how saints, through their holy lives, become vibrant canvases upon which God's artistry is magnificently displayed.

The concept of holiness as an art form begins with the understanding that each life is a raw material, a potential masterpiece awaiting the touch of the divine artist. Saints are those souls who, through their openness to God's grace, have been transformed into exquisite manifestations of spiritual beauty. Their lives are testimonies to the sublime craftsmanship of God, who carves virtues in the human heart as a sculptor shapes his creations.

At the heart of this divine artistry lies the profound alliance between human free will and divine grace. Saints, in their journey towards holiness, collaborate with God, allowing His grace to mold their beings into symbols of His love and mercy. This partnership mirrors the relationship between an artist and his medium, where the final output is neither solely the work of the artist nor entirely the property of the material, but a harmonious creation that transcends both.

It's essential to recognize that the making of a saint, much like the process of creating art, involves moments of both sublime inspiration and profound struggle. The path to sainthood is often strewn with trials and tribulations, which, when embraced with faith, act as chisels and brushes in God's hands, refining and defining the soul's contours. Saints embrace these challenges, not as hindrances but as opportunities for grace to further shape their lives into holy masterpieces.

The diversity in the saints' backgrounds, experiences, and paths to holiness underscores the universal call to sanctity and the unique manner in which each soul can reflect God's beauty. Just as different art forms - painting, sculpture, music - reveal various facets of beauty, so too do saints manifest the multiplicity of God's grace in human life. From the austere beauty of the desert fathers to the vibrant lives of modern saints, each reveals a distinct hue on the spectrum of sanctity.

Holiness, therefore, can be seen as the ultimate artistic vocation, wherein the soul, in collaboration with divine grace, works towards the masterpiece of its sanctification. Saints exemplify the pinnacle of this sacred art, inviting all to partake in the creative process of becoming reflections of divine beauty.

The veneration of saints in the Catholic tradition is not merely an act of reverence but a recognition of their role as conduits of divine inspiration. Through their intercessions, saints continue to influence the living canvas of the Church, guiding the faithful in their artistic and spiritual journeys. Moreover, by meditating on the lives of saints, believers can glean insights into the art of living a life pleasing to God.

Contemplating the lives of saints thus becomes an exercise in aesthetic appreciation and spiritual formation, highlighting the indissoluble link between beauty, creativity, and sanctity. As masterpieces of God's handiwork, saints inspire both admiration and emulation, challenging all to embrace the artistry of living a holy life.

The portrayal of saints in Catholic art further illuminates their role as divine masterpieces. Throughout history, artists have been captivated by the beauty of sanctity, endeavoring to capture the essence of holiness through their works. From medieval iconography to Renaissance paintings, the artistic depictions of saints not only serve as visual catechesis but also as mediums through which the mystery of divine grace is communicated.

Moreover, saints themselves have been patrons and creators of art, understanding the power of beauty as a pathway to the divine. Saints like St. John of Damascus defended the veneration of icons, while others, such as St. Hildegard of Bingen, created music and poetry that continue to inspire. Their artistic contributions underscore the intrinsic connection between creativity and spirituality, affirming the role of art as a vehicle of divine revelation.

In conclusion, the art of holiness is a dynamic interplay between divine grace and human response, a collaborative effort in which the soul allows itself to be sculpted by God's loving hands. Saints, as the ultimate embodiments of this sacred art, beckon all to the adventure of sanctity, revealing that the path to holiness is not only a journey of spiritual ascent but also an act of creative expression, inviting each to become co-artists with God in the masterpiece of their lives.

By exploring the lives of saints through the lens of art, believers are reminded that holiness is not an abstract ideal but a tangible, vibrant reality, accessible to all who open themselves to the grace of God. The saints, in their celestial beauty, thus serve as beacons of hope, guiding the faithful towards the ultimate Source of all beauty and creativity.

As we journey through the rich tapestry of Catholic tradition, may we be inspired by the art of holiness embodied in the lives of the saints, allowing their example to shape our path towards sanctity. In doing so, we participate in the divine artistry of God, contributing our own strokes to the ever-unfolding masterpiece of creation.

Patron Saints of the Arts In the divine tapestry that is the history and practice of Catholic art, a brilliant thread that consistently emerges is the veneration of certain saints who have been designated as patrons of the arts. This recognition is not merely an act of pious remembrance but a profound acknowledgment of the spiritual dimension inherent in the creation and appreciation of art. It is in these saints that artists across generations have found companionship, guidance, and intercession as they navigate the sacred act of creation.

The notion of patron saints serving as heavenly advocates is deeply embedded in Catholic tradition. It is a reflection of the belief in the communion of saints, a doctrine asserting the spiritual solidarity among the faithful, both living and deceased. This communion envisages a continuous interplay of prayer and support, extending beyond the terrestrial realm into the celestial. Artists, in their quest to manifest the divine through the material, often encounter unique challenges that make the support of patron saints not merely desirable but essential.

Among the most venerated patrons of the arts is Saint Luke the Evangelist. Tradition holds that Saint Luke was not only a chronicler of the Gospel but also a painter, responsible for creating the first icons of the Virgin Mary and the Christ Child. His patronage extends over painters and visual artists, embodying the sacred duty to depict the divine mysteries with reverence and skill.

Saint Luke's example acts as a beacon, guiding artists to perceive and portray the spiritual truth lying beyond the visible world.

Another illustrious figure is Saint Cecilia, the patroness of musicians. Legend has it that Cecilia sang in her heart to the Lord even as she faced martyrdom, a testament to her unshakeable faith and devotion. Musicians of all forms look to Saint Cecilia as an exemplar of the transcendent power of music to elevate the soul and communicate the ineffable. In her, they find the courage to embrace their calling, creating sounds that echo the harmonies of heaven.

Saint John the Evangelist holds a unique place as the patron of theologians and writers. His Gospel and epistles penetrate deeply into the mysteries of the Word made flesh, communicating sublime theological truths through the written word. Authors, poets, and scholars see in Saint John a model for their own endeavors to articulate the truths of the faith, striving to illuminate the Word in the hearts and minds of their readers.

Architecture, the art that combines functionality with aesthetic to create spaces for worship and community, finds a patron in Saint Barbara. According to her legend, she added three windows to a bathhouse to symbolize the Holy Trinity, an act of devotion that led to her martyrdom. Architects and builders look up to her as they design physical structures that reflect the beauty of the divine architect.

The realm of sculpture is watched over by Saint Phidias, though lesser-known, his legacy as a sculptor of ancient Greece symbolizes the bridging of classical artistry with Christian themes, enriching the Church's visual heritage. Sculptors seek his intercession as they chisel and mold raw materials into forms that evoke the divine presence.

Art educators and students find a patron in Saint Catherine of Bologna, herself an accomplished artist, as well as a learned nun. Saint Catherine authored treatises on art and spirituality, blending her artistic talent with deep spiritual insight. Educators and students alike invoke her guidance to balance technical mastery with soulful expression.

Dance, an art form that communicates through the movement of the body, looks to King David as its patron. The biblical account of David dancing before the Ark of the Covenant with all his might celebrates the joyous expression of faith through bodily movement. Dancers find in David a figure who sanctifies their art, encouraging them to use their entire being in the adoration of God.

In the pursuit of any artistic endeavor, challenges are inevitable. Yet, in the communion with the saints, Catholic artists discover a reservoir of inspiration and intercession. These holy men and women, who once walked the earth and engaged in the act of creation themselves, continue to participate in the Church's life through their example and their prayers.

The intercession of patron saints is a source of comfort and strength, offering artists a spiritual foundation upon which to build their work. It is through this heavenly fellowship that the beauty of Catholic art finds its deepest resonance, grounded not only in human skill and creativity but in the divine inspiration that animates all true art.

As artists engage with their craft, they do so in the company of saints who understand the intrinsic challenges and joys of artistic creation. This companionship across time and space is a testament to the universality and timelessness of both art and faith. It reaffirms the artist's role in the divine economy of salvation, where talents are nurtured and deployed for the greater glory of God and the sanctification of the world.

Ultimately, the patron saints of the arts stand as luminous examples of how the integration of faith and art can elevate the human spirit, drawing it closer to the divine. In every brushstroke, note, and word, artists are invited to enter into a dialogue with the divine, co-creating with God to reveal the splendor of His creation and the depth of His love for humanity.

In this sacred endeavor, the Church calls upon the patron saints of the arts not simply as distant figures of reverence but as present and active participants in the ongoing creation of beauty. They remind us that art, in all its forms, is a vital expression of the human response to God's inexhaustible goodness and beauty, a response that encompasses both the creator and the beholder.

Therefore, to all who partake in the creation, study, or appreciation of art under the vast umbrella of the Catholic tradition, the patron saints extend their encouragement, guidance, and intercessory prayer. Their examples stand as a testament to the profound union between divine grace and human creativity, a synergy that bears fruit in the splendid variety of Catholic art, enriching the Church and the world with its beauty.

Chapter 8: Science and Faith: A Catholic Integration

The interplay of science and faith within the Catholic tradition has established a rich tapestry that extends far beyond the simplistic narrative of conflict. This synergy is not merely a contemporary rapprochement but is deeply rooted in the intellectual and spiritual foundation of the Church. Indeed, the very endeavor of scientific pursuit has been animated and enriched by a faith perspective that sees the natural world as a testament to the Creator's genius.

In tracing the contributions of Catholic scientists, one finds a lineage of scholars whose work was not only groundbreaking in the scientific field but also deeply illuminated by their faith. These individuals saw no contradiction between their rigorous inquiry into the natural world and their profound allegiance to the divine. From the genetic monk, Gregor Mendel, to the father of modern geology, Nicolas Steno, Catholic scientists have consistently demonstrated that faith and reason are not adversaries but allies in the quest for understanding.

The integration of science and Catholic faith finds a robust foundation in the Church's teaching that God is the author of all truth. This principle entails that the pursuit of scientific knowledge, far from being antithetical to faith, is a path to deeper theological insight. The natural laws, in their elegance and predictability, reflect a cosmos that is intelligible and designed, pointing beyond itself to a transcendent Creator.

Furthermore, the Catholic intellectual tradition, particularly through Thomism, provides a philosophical framework that welcomes the contributions of science. This philosophical approach does not relegate faith to the realm of the irrational but rather understands faith and reason as two dimensions of a coherent truth-seeking endeavor. Theological truths and scientific discoveries are seen as complementary, each providing unique insights into the reality of existence.

One quintessential example of the harmony between science and religion is found in the work of Georges Lemaître, a Catholic priest and physicist who proposed the Big Bang theory. Lemaître's groundbreaking theory, which is now a cornerstone of contemporary cosmology, demonstrates how individuals of faith have not only participated in the scientific enterprise but have led some of its most pivotal developments.

The Catholic Church's engagement with the scientific community, advocating for ethical responsibility in scientific research, underscores a shared commitment to the dignity of human life and the stewardship of creation. This engagement is rooted in the belief that scientific advancements should serve the common good and be informed by moral principles.

This integration of science and faith is also profoundly reflected in Catholic education. Catholic universities and schools worldwide strive to provide an education that bridges the gap between science and spirituality, promoting an understanding of science that is enriched by faith. Through this holistic approach, students are encouraged to appreciate the scientific endeavor not only as an intellectual pursuit but as a spiritual journey that reveals the depth and wonder of creation.

The dialogue between science and faith is further enriched by the Church's social teaching, which offers a vision of the human person and the universe that is deeply consonant with the ethical dimensions of science. This teaching emphasizes the interconnectedness of all creation and the responsibility of human beings to act as custodians of the environment, a stance that resonates with contemporary concerns about sustainability and ecological justice.

In the realm of bioethics, the Catholic faith provides critical perspectives on the implications of scientific advancements, such as genetic engineering and artificial intelligence. These perspectives are grounded in a theological anthropology that values the inherent dignity of every human being and the sanctity of life. Such viewpoints contribute to a broader ethical discourse, highlighting the need for a moral compass in navigating the complex questions posed by scientific progress.

Art, as a reflection of the divine, often celebrates the mysteries uncovered by science. Catholic art has the unique capacity to capture the awe and wonder of the universe, bridging the gap between empirical observation and spiritual contemplation. This integration is a testimony to the Catholic imagination, which sees the handiwork of God in the empirical and the transcendent.

Yet, the relationship between science and faith is not without its challenges. Historical episodes, such as the Galileo affair, remind us of the tensions that can arise when institutions fail to recognize the autonomy and legitimacy of scientific inquiry. These episodes, however, have also been occasions for reflection and growth, leading to a more nuanced understanding of the science-faith interface within the Church.

In conclusion, the Catholic integration of science and faith is not a mere accommodation but a profound recognition of the complementarity of these realms of human knowledge. This integration invites a deeper exploration of the world, informed by the conviction that all truth, whether revealed through Scripture or discovered through science, ultimately leads to the same divine source.

The exploration of the universe, in all its vastness and complexity, thus becomes an act of worship, a testament to the Creator whose existence and attributes are reflected in the order and beauty of His creation. In this shared journey of discovery, science and faith offer distinct yet converging paths to understanding the mystery and majesty of the cosmos.

The profound harmony between science and the Catholic faith embodies a hopeful vision for the future—a future in which the pursuit of knowledge, guided by ethical and spiritual wisdom, contributes to the flourishing of humanity and the greater glory of God.

Contributions of Catholic Scientists

In the vast tapestry of human discovery, Catholic scientists have stitched vivid threads, marrying the meticulous pursuit of scientific knowledge with a profound spiritual insight. Within the chapter of history, these intellectual pioneers have shown that the realms of science and faith are not disparate territories, but rather intertwined paths leading to the same ultimate truth.

Historically, the Church has played a pivotal role as the cradle of scientific advancement. Monastic communities, with their methodical approach to study and replication, laid the groundwork for the empirical method. It is within these hallowed halls that men of faith first sought to understand the workings of the natural world, not as a challenge to the divine, but as an exploration of God's handiwork.

Consider the towering figure of Nicolaus Copernicus, a Renaissance mathematician and astronomer who proposed a heliocentric model of the universe. Contrary to popular narrative, his groundbreaking work, *De revolutionibus orbium coelestium*, was received with interest by the Catholic Church at the time. Copernicus's dedication to uncovering the mysteries of the celestial spheres was rooted in his deep-seated belief in a Creator of harmonious order.

Following in these monumental footsteps, Gregor Mendel, an Augustinian friar, laid the foundations for modern genetics through his meticulous cross-breeding experiments on pea plants. Mendel's work, which today forms the cornerstone of biological inheritance studies, sprang from a place of faith-fueled curiosity about the laws governing God's creation.

In the field of physics, the Jesuit priest and scientist Roger Boscovich is lauded for his contributions to atomic theory and the theory of forces. Boscovich's scientific endeavors were driven by a desire to understand the underlying principles of the universe, reflecting a deeper contemplation of the divine architecture.

The integration of faith and science reaches a profound crescendo in the life and work of Georges Lemaître, a Belgian priest and astrophysicist. Lemaître was the first to propose the theory of the expansion of the universe, now renowned as the Big Bang theory. His hypothesis brought to the fore the concept of a universe with a singular beginning, resonating with the metaphysical quest for a First Cause.

These Catholic scientists, and many others, pursued their inquiries under the gaze of a Creator, believing that to study the natural world was to unveil the language of God written in the book of creation. Their work exemplifies an integration wherein scientific exploration serves as an act of worship, a dedication of one's intellect to glorifying the Creator.

The Church has recognized the profound value of scientific pursuit, illustrated by the establishment of the Vatican Observatory in the late 16th century. This enduring institution symbolizes the Catholic commitment to advancing human understanding of the cosmos, underscoring the belief that faith and reason are not only compatible but complementary.

Furthermore, the Pontifical Academy of Sciences, composed of eminent scientists from various fields, including Nobel laureates, stands as testament to the Church's support for scientific inquiry. This body continues to explore critical issues at the nexus of science and ethics, emphasizing the moral implications of scientific advancements.

The contributions of Catholic scientists have also extended to ethical discussions in science, particularly in the realms of genetics and bioethics. They champion the cause of human dignity and the sanctity of life, reminding the scientific community of its responsibility towards ethical considerations.

This legacy of Catholic scientists serves not only as a testament to the Church's role in the development of the sciences but also as a reminder of the unity of truth. The pursuit of scientific knowledge, when undertaken with a heart turned towards the divine, enriches both the mind and the spirit.

In the modern age, where the dichotomy between science and faith is often emphasized, the examples of these faithful scientists offer a compelling narrative of integration. They remind us that in the quest for understanding the natural world, there is space for wonder, worship, and a deeper comprehension of our place within God's creation.

As the church moves forward, it continues to foster an environment where scientific inquiry and faith dialogue enrich each other. Encouraging a new generation of Catholic scientists to explore, question, and discover with an ethos that seeks to integrate their spiritual beliefs with their scientific work stands as a beacon of hope for the future.

In conclusion, the contributions of Catholic scientists throughout history serve as a bridge between the empirical and the divine, inviting all to a deeper consideration of the world as a coherent, interconnected whole. Their legacy is a testament to the church's belief in the harmony of all truth and the profound role of scientific endeavor in the unfolding story of creation.

The Harmony between Science and Religion

In the modern era, where the chasm between science and religion often seems insurmountable, the Catholic tradition stands as a testament to the profound unity that can exist between these realms of human pursuit. The Catholic faith, with its rich intellectual heritage, offers a vision of harmony where science and religion are not antagonistic but complementary paths towards understanding the fullness of truth. This perspective is not merely academic but is deeply embedded in the Catholic approach to art, revealing how scientific discovery and faith can together inspire a more profound appreciation of beauty and truth in the world around us.

The narrative that science and religion are at odds is a relatively recent development in the long history of human inquiry. For centuries, Catholic thinkers have been at the forefront of scientific exploration, viewing their work as a means of uncovering the intricacies of God's creation. From great minds like Copernicus, who was a canon of the church, to Mendel, a monk who laid the foundation for modern genetics, Catholic scientists have demonstrated that faith and scientific endeavor can coexist harmoniously, each illuminating the other.

This convergence of science and religion within the Catholic intellectual tradition is grounded in the understanding of the cosmos as a creation of God, a creation that is fundamentally good and intelligible. Thus, the pursuit of scientific knowledge is seen as a way to honor God by exploring the wonders of His creation, and through this exploration, artists and scientists alike can draw closer to the Divine. This perspective invites a dialogue between science and faith, suggesting that one can inform and enrich the understanding of the other.

The interplay between science and religion can be vividly seen in the realm of Catholic art. The beauty of the natural world, so meticulously uncovered by scientists, has been a source of inspiration for countless artists seeking to express the majesty of the Creator through their work. The intricate details of a flower, the vastness of the night sky, the complex patterns found in the human body - all speak of a divine order and have found their echoes in cathedrals, paintings, and hymns, inviting the observer into a deeper contemplation of God's presence in the world.

In this synthesis of science and religion, the role of the artist becomes that of a bridge-builder, connecting the empirical with the spiritual, the observable with the invisible. By drawing on the insights of science, the artist can create works that not only reflect the beauty of the created world but also evoke a sense of wonder and awe that points beyond the material to the ultimate Creator. This role is crucial in a world where the empirical often overshadows the mystical, reminding society of the deeper mysteries that lie beyond the reach of microscopes and telescopes.

The harmony between science and religion in the Catholic tradition also serves as a powerful antidote to the materialism and reductionism that often characterize contemporary thought. In a culture that frequently reduces reality to what can be measured and quantified, the Catholic synthesis opens a window to the transcendent, asserting the existence of realities that surpass material confines. This perspective does not diminish the value of scientific inquiry but rather enhances it, imbuing it with a sense of purpose that transcends mere utilitarianism.

This integral view of science and faith has profound implications for how we understand the human person. Catholic teaching, informed by both faith and reason, asserts the dignity and sacredness of human life, rooted in the belief that every person is made in the image of God. This understanding challenges the reductionist view of humanity often found in certain branches of science and instead invites a holistic view of human existence that values the spiritual, intellectual, and physical dimensions of the person.

In the contemporary quest for sustainability and ecological responsibility, the Catholic vision of the harmony between science and religion offers critical insights. The scientific study of our environment, coupled with a religious sense of stewardship for creation, provides a compelling framework for addressing the environmental challenges of our time. Pope Francis' encyclical, *Laudato Si'*, exemplifies this approach, calling for an "integral ecology" that respects both human dignity and the integrity of creation.

The journey towards integrating science and religion is not without its challenges. Misunderstandings, biases, and historical conflicts have, at times, strained this relationship. However, the Catholic Church continues to advocate for a dialogue between these realms, understanding that both are essential for the well-being of humanity and the pursuit of truth. The Pontifical Academy of Sciences, for example, symbolizes the Church's commitment to engaging with the scientific community, encouraging research and discussion on issues of mutual interest.

In the realm of education, Catholic institutions play a pivotal role in fostering the harmony between science and religion. Through a curriculum that embraces both faith and reason, students are encouraged to see these domains not as isolated silos but as complementary ways of understanding the world and their place within it. Such an education cultivates a more integrated view of knowledge, preparing individuals to navigate the complexities of modern life with wisdom and integrity.

As we look to the future, the intersection of science and religion in the Catholic tradition offers a hopeful vision for humanity. In a world that yearns for meaning and unity, the Catholic synthesis provides a model for reconciling disparate elements of human experience, suggesting that faith and reason, together, can lead us to a more profound understanding of our place in the cosmos. This unity, reflected in the beauty of Catholic art and thought, continues to inspire those who seek to explore the depths of reality, guided by the light of faith and the tools of scientific inquiry.

In conclusion, the harmony between science and religion within the Catholic tradition is not a forced amalgamation but a natural convergence of paths that lead to truth. By embracing both the empirical and the spiritual, Catholics are invited to participate in a grand adventure of discovery, where the mysteries of faith and the findings of science coalesce into a deeper understanding of the divine tapestry that is our universe. It is in this sacred space, where the truths of science and the mysteries of faith intertwine, that the Catholic artist finds the inspiration to create works that transcend time, echoing the eternal beauty of the Creator.

Chapter 9: The Moral Imagination: Ethics and the Catholic Artist

The confluence of morality and creativity crafts a distinct beacon for artists within the Catholic tradition. The indelible pursuit of beauty, intertwined with the aspiration for the divine, marks a pathway laden with ethical considerations for the Catholic artist. To engage in the creation of art is to embark on a dialogue not only with the world but with the very essence of faith and moral understanding. This chapter delves into the profound relationship between art as a medium for moral teaching and the responsibilities that burgeon from this unique convergence.

Art, in its myriad forms, serves as a vessel for expressing the ineffable, for bridging the chasm between the divine and the earthly. Through the lens of the Catholic faith, art becomes a pivotal medium for moral teaching, where the embodiment of virtues and the portrayal of truths transcend mere representation. The Catholic artist, therefore, shoulders a formidable responsibility, to illuminate the path of righteousness and to kindle the flames of moral imagination within the hearts of the beholder.

The challenges faced by artists in this sacred vocation are manifold. The modern era, with its rapidly evolving cultural landscapes, presents a mélange of ethical dilemmas and temptations that can potentially obscure the moral compass. Navigating through the quandaries of artistic expression, while adhering to the tenets of the

Catholic faith, requires a resolute adherence to principles that are often countercultural. The Catholic artist must thus, engage in a delicate balancing act, forging creations that resonate with contemporary sensibilities while remaining steadfast to eternal verities.

The task at hand, though daunting, is not insurmountable. Historical precedence furnishes a rich tapestry of Catholic artists who have adeptly married their creative endeavors with their spiritual convictions, crafting works that not only enchant the aesthetic sense but also elevate the soul. From the ethereal melodies of Gregorian chant to the visual splendors of the Sistine Chapel, the Catholic artistic heritage stands as a testament to the power of art to evoke a deeper contemplation of the moral and the divine.

Within this venerable tradition, art transcends its physical form, serving as a conduit for spiritual enlightenment and moral reflection. The Catholic artist engages in a creative process that is both reflective and active, a process that seeks to imbue the material world with a glimpse of the divine splendor. It is here, in the act of creation, that the artist becomes a steward of God's grace, channeling their talents towards the glorification of the creator and the sanctification of the world.

The moral imagination of the Catholic artist thus emerges as a pivotal force, one that has the capacity to reshape societal norms and to forge a more illuminated path forward. In crafting narratives, images, and sounds that reflect the richness of the Catholic faith, the artist imbarks on a mission to awaken the conscience, to challenge complacency, and to inspire a quest for truth and beauty. It is a mission that demands not only talent but also courage, integrity, and a profound sense of purpose.

Engaging with contemporary issues through the prism of faith and morality, the Catholic artist plays a crucial role in articulating a vision of the world that transcends mere surface appearances. By drawing upon the wealth of theological and ethical insights that characterize the Catholic tradition, artists have the unique opportunity to contribute to a culture that values transcendence, nurtures the human spirit, and champions the dignity of every person.

As we consider the path of the Catholic artist, it becomes clear that the vocation is imbued with a profound societal implication. In an age marked by relativism and a fleeting regard for the sacred, the Catholic artist's engagement with moral themes offers a counter-narrative, one that reasserts the relevance of faith and ethics in the public square. It is in this engagement that the potential for transformation lies, both within the heart of the artist and within the hearts of those touched by their work.

Conclusively, the moral imagination of the Catholic artist is not a mere adjunct to their creative ability; it is the very wellspring from which their artistry draws its deepest significance. In harnessing this imagination, the Catholic artist becomes a herald of hope, a beacon of beauty, and a guardian of the sacred, whose work not only delights the senses but also calls us to a higher way of being.

As we delve further into the nuances of this noble calling, let us remember that the art we create is not for our glory, but for the greater glory of God. It is through our creative endeavors that we partake in the divine act of creation, and through our moral imagination that we illuminate the path toward truth, goodness, and beauty.

Art as a Medium for Moral Teaching

At the heart of Catholic tradition lies a profound recognition of art's capacity to convey moral and spiritual truths. The Catholic artist, much like a gardener of the human soul, is tasked with an endeavor of eternal significance: to wield creativity as an instrument for moral teaching. The convergence of beauty and truth in Catholic art is not merely aesthetic; it serves a deeply educative purpose, guiding the soul towards contemplation of the divine.

The philosophical underpinnings of this thought can be traced back to the notion of the 'moral imagination.' The moral imagination enables individuals to perceive and appreciate the moral dimensions of life, not through abstract ethical principles but through the concrete, embodied realities depicted in art. The stories, images, and symbols presented in Catholic art serve as vessels through which moral truths are communicated, inviting the beholder to venture beyond the surface and engage with the deeper spiritual lessons.

In the creation of sacred art, the artist enters into a dialogue with the divine, acting as a mediator between God and humanity. Through their works, Catholic artists offer a window into the transcendent, portraying scenes of virtue, sacrifice, redemption, and salvation. These themes resonate with the human experience, offering solace and inspiration, challenging viewers to reflect on their own moral choices.

The historical testimony of the Church's commitment to art as a medium for moral teaching is evident in the cathedrals, paintings, sculptures, and liturgical music that have been preserved through the ages. These masterpieces of sacred art are not only treasures of religious devotion but also moral compasses, guiding the faithful towards the good, the true, and the beautiful. They encapsulate the essence of Catholic moral teaching, embodying the virtues and values that define a life lived in accordance with God's will.

However, the responsibility bestowed upon the Catholic artist is fraught with challenges. In an era where secular ideologies often overshadow spiritual values, the task of creating art that resonates with both aesthetic and moral integrity is daunting. Artists must navigate the delicate balance between artistic freedom and fidelity to the teachings of the Church, ensuring that their work uplifts rather than undermines the moral imagination of the viewer.

To address these challenges, Catholic artists are called to cultivate a deep spiritual life, rooted in prayer and sacramental practice. It is only by connecting with the source of all beauty—God himself—that artists can hope to create works that truly enlighten and elevate the soul. This spiritual orientation ensures that the artist remains attuned to the moral dimension of their creative endeavors, striving always to glorify God and edify the human heart.

Moreover, the Church plays a pivotal role in nurturing the moral imagination through art. By fostering a culture of appreciation for sacred art and supporting the endeavors of Catholic artists, the Church can ensure that art continues to serve as a vibrant medium for moral teaching. Educational initiatives, commissions of new works, and the preservation of the artistic heritage are essential in this regard, empowering artists to contribute to the moral and spiritual renewal of society.

The impact of art as a medium for moral teaching extends beyond the confines of the Church, reaching out to the broader society. In a world hungering for meaning and direction, Catholic art offers a beacon of hope, illuminating the path towards a more compassionate, just, and virtuous society. It calls upon all individuals, regardless of their faith background, to contemplate the deeper realities of existence, encouraging a collective pursuit of the good.

In conclusion, the role of art in Catholic moral teaching is indispensable. It enriches the moral imagination, inspires virtue, and leads the soul towards contemplation of the divine mysteries. As stewards of this sacred tradition, Catholic artists are entrusted with a noble mission: to harness the power of beauty in the service of truth, guiding humanity towards the eternal embrace of God's love.

Challenges and Responsibilities In the realm of Catholic art, where the divine intertwines with the tangible, artists encounter a unique set of challenges and bear profound responsibilities. Their work is not merely a matter of personal expression but an act of worship and a medium for evangelization. The path they tread, one that seeks to embody eternal truths within temporal forms, is fraught with both obstacles and opportunities for deep spiritual engagement and societal transformation.

To illuminate the gravity and grandeur of their calling, it is essential to consider the multifaceted challenges that Catholic artists face. The first, and perhaps most daunting, is the challenge of representing the ineffable. How does one give form to the formless, or portray the sacred mysteries that transcend human comprehension? This task requires an artist to delve deeply into the wellspring of faith, drawing inspiration from the rich traditions of the Church while invoking the guidance of the Holy Spirit.

Furthermore, in a world increasingly characterized by secularism and materialism, Catholic artists encounter the challenge of communication. The symbols and narratives once universally understood now speak to an audience that may be unfamiliar with, or indifferent to, the spiritual realities they represent. Artists must, therefore, cultivate a language of beauty that transcends cultural and religious boundaries, inviting all observers into a shared experience of the transcendent.

The responsibility accompanying this challenge is immense. Catholic artists must ensure that their work adheres to the truth of the Gospel, embodying the Gospel's teachings not only in content but in form. A misrepresentation or trivialization of the faith can lead not only to confusion but also to scandal, distancing viewers from the Church rather than drawing them nearer.

Moreover, the call to create is also a call to humility and service. In an age where the artist is often celebrated as a visionary or revolutionary, the Catholic artist is reminded that their creativity is a gift from God, meant to serve God's people and glorify His name. Their work is an act of stewardship over the talents entrusted to them, requiring both a recognition of their limits and a relentless pursuit of excellence.

This stewardship extends to the material world as well. The responsible use of resources, the ethical treatment of subjects, and the intentionality behind each work of art reflect the artist's reverence for creation and Creator alike. In this, the Catholic artist models a countercultural approach to art, one that values integrity over notoriety and the communal over the individualistic.

The Catholic artist also faces the internal challenge of balancing faith and creativity. The tension between artistic freedom and adherence to doctrinal truths can be a fruitful source of innovation but can also lead to conflict and self-doubt. Navigating this tension requires a deep personal relationship with God and an ongoing engagement with the Church's teachings and traditions.

Another significant challenge lies in the realm of reception. An artist must be prepared for the possibility that their work will be misunderstood, criticized, or ignored. This reality demands a resilience rooted not in ego or acclaim but in the conviction that their work ultimately serves a higher purpose. The Catholic artist's responsibility here is to listen, discern, and, where necessary, engage in dialogue with both critics and supporters, always with charity and truth.

The challenge of accessibility is also paramount. Catholic art should not be confined to sacred spaces or elite circles but should reach out to the marginalized and the searching. This inclusivity requires both creativity in dissemination and a sensitivity to the diverse ways in which people encounter and interpret art.

Moreover, in a rapidly evolving digital landscape, Catholic artists are called to innovate, bringing the timeless beauty of the faith into new mediums and platforms. The potential for evangelization in this space is vast but so are the risks of dilution and distortion. Navigating these waters demands a judicious combination of boldness and prudence.

The responsibility of mentorship is another critical dimension. Seasoned artists have a duty to guide and inspire the next generation, imparting not only skills and techniques but also a spiritual and moral framework within which to create. This transmission of knowledge and wisdom ensures the vitality and continuity of Catholic art.

Lastly, there is the challenge of personal sanctity. The Catholic artist is called to a life of holiness, reflecting in their conduct the beauty and truth they seek to express in their work. This journey towards sanctity is both the foundation and the fruit of their labor, demanding ongoing conversion and a deep communion with the Church and her sacraments.

In conclusion, the challenges and responsibilities of Catholic artists are indeed profound, touching upon every aspect of their personal and professional lives. Yet, it is precisely through engaging with these challenges, fortified by faith and guided by the Church, that artists fulfill their vocation. Their work becomes a beacon of beauty and truth in a world desperately in need of both, a testament to the transformative power of art when rooted in the divine.

Chapter 10: Politics and the Catholic Conscience

The realm of politics is often seen as a secular domain, a sphere distant from the spiritual and the sacred. Yet, the teachings of the Catholic Church assert that no aspect of human life is outside God's care and concern, including politics. The Catholic conscience, informed by a rich tradition of social teaching, provides a moral compass in navigating the complexities of political life. This chapter explores the intricate dance between politics and the Catholic conscience, revealing how Catholic social teachings and artistic expressions of justice and peace serve not just as guidelines but as a call to action for the faithful.

In the heart of Catholic teaching is a profound emphasis on the dignity of the human person. This foundational belief shapes how Catholics engage with political issues, advocating for policies that protect and uplift the inherent worth of every individual. This vision extends to the realms of economics, healthcare, education, and the environment, asserting a preferential option for the poor and vulnerable. As Catholics, our political engagement is not driven by partisan ideologies but by the Gospel's demand for love, mercy, and justice.

The influence of Catholic social teaching on the political sphere is undeniable. From the seminal encyclical *Rerum Novarum* to the recent writings of Pope Francis, the Church has consistently voiced its concern for social justice, the common good, and the stewardship of creation. These documents serve not as mere academic discourses but as urgent calls to action, challenging both individuals and communities to transform society in the light of the Gospel.

Artistic expressions of justice and peace have a unique power to move hearts and inspire action. Throughout history, Catholic artists have used their talents to critique the injustices of their times and to envision a world more reflective of God's kingdom. From the prophetic sculptures and paintings calling for peace and reformation to contemporary works highlighting the plight of refugees and the marginalized, Catholic art serves as a powerful conduit for social and political commentary.

The intersection of politics and the Catholic conscience is also a space for dialogue and collaboration. Recognizing the complexity of political life, the Church advocates for a culture of encounter, where diverse voices are heard and respected. Catholics are encouraged to engage in respectful debate, to listen deeply to the experiences of others, and to seek common ground in the pursuit of justice and peace.

However, navigating the political sphere as a Catholic is not without its challenges. In a world marked by polarization and conflict, Catholics often find themselves caught between competing ideologies. The Church's teachings sometimes challenge the platforms of all political parties, reminding Catholics that their ultimate allegiance is not to a temporal power but to God's eternal kingdom. This tension serves as a reminder that the journey of faith involves constant discernment, prayer, and the courage to speak truth to power.

In conclusion, the relationship between politics and the Catholic conscience is complex and multifaceted. It is an invitation to deep reflection, discernment, and action, guided by the principles of Catholic social teaching. In this interplay, art emerges as a potent force for societal change, offering visions of hope and solidarity. As Catholics, our political engagement is a testament to our faith in action, an embodiment of our call to be leaven in the world, working tirelessly for the Kingdom of God.

The Influence of Catholic Social Teaching

The intricate tapestry of Catholic social teaching, woven with threads of justice, peace, and human dignity, casts a profound influence on the political sphere, where the Catholic conscience is called to act decisively and with compassion. At the heart of this teaching lies a compelling vision of the common good, a principle that finds resonance in the political arena as Catholics strive to imbue governance with values that reflect the kingdom of God.

Catholic social teaching, with its rich historical roots and evolving understanding, shapes the political conscience through a clear call to prioritize the marginalized and the poor. This is not merely an invitation but a moral imperative, driving Catholics into the political realm armed with a mission to transform societies in the image of divine justice. The foundational document "Rerum Novarum," issued by Pope Leo XIII, marked a significant milestone in articulating the church's response to the social challenges of the day, setting a precedent for active Catholic engagement in political and social issues (Pope Leo XIII, 1891).

Integral to Catholic social teaching is the principle of solidarity. This notion extends beyond simple empathy or temporary compassion toward those in distress; it signifies a deep, enduring, and active commitment to the well-being of all, recognizing the interconnectedness of humanity. Solidarity compels Catholics to view political engagement not as a realm of power struggles but as a platform for service, where the elevation of human dignity is paramount.

The respect for human life, from conception to natural death, is another cornerstone that guides the political conscience informed by Catholic social teaching. This comprehensive approach to the sanctity of life challenges the political and social structures that perpetuate inequality, war, poverty, and disregard for the environment. It inspires a politics that cherishes life in all its forms, fostering a culture that upholds the inherent dignity bestowed upon every human being by their Creator.

The principle of subsidiarity is central to Catholic political thought, advocating for decisions to be made at the lowest appropriate level to ensure they adequately reflect the needs and aspirations of the community involved. This principle encourages a vibrant and participatory democracy, where local knowledge and wisdom guide the political process, and the excessive centralization of power is avoided.

Catholic social teaching also urges a re-evaluation of the role of property and resources, emphasizing their status as gifts entrusted to humanity for the common good. This perspective challenges unbridled capitalism and consumerism, calling for an economic system that serves the human person rather than the reverse. It propels Catholics into political advocacy for policies that ensure just distribution of the world's goods, enabling every person to live in dignity and freedom.

The care for God's creation, integral to Catholic social doctrine, shapes a political conscience that seeks to combat the environmental crises of our time. This ecological dimension calls Catholics to stewardship of the earth, promoting sustainable policies that protect and restore the natural world for future generations. It is a call to transition from exploitation to preservation, recognizing the sacredness of all creation.

In the face of globalization, Catholic social teaching addresses the challenges and opportunities presented by our interconnected world. It calls for a globalization of solidarity, where the global economy serves the human family and where the barriers that divide humanity are overcome through compassion, understanding, and cooperation.

The preferential option for the poor, a guiding principle of Catholic social teaching, demands a political commitment to policies and practices that uplift those marginalized by society. It challenges the structures of sin that perpetuate poverty and inequality, urging Catholics to become voices for the voiceless in the political sphere.

The pursuit of peace stands as a central objective, guiding Catholics toward advocacy for disarmament, conflict resolution, and reconciliation. Catholic social teaching envisions a world where dialogue triumphs over discord, and where justice lays the groundwork for lasting peace.

Religious freedom, a fundamental human right, is ardently defended in Catholic social teaching, recognizing the critical role of faith in the personal and social lives of individuals. This principle calls Catholics to safeguard the right to religious expression for all, advocating for policies that ensure freedom of worship and that respect the moral and spiritual dimensions of human life.

The prophetic vision presented by Catholic social teaching invites Catholics to embrace a holistic approach to politics—one that transcends partisan divisions and seeks the flourishing of all humanity. It is a call to live out the Gospel in public life, bringing the light of Christ into the discussions, decisions, and policies that shape our world.

As Catholics engage with the political realm, guided by the profound insights of Catholic social teaching, they serve as leaven in society, striving to mold the temporal order in accordance with divine law. It is a mission that demands courage, compassion, and unwavering commitment to the dignity of every person, reflecting the love of God in the political arena.

In conclusion, the influence of Catholic social teaching on politics is transformative, challenging Catholics to be agents of change who advocate for a society marked by justice, peace, and the integral development of the human person. It is a testament to the enduring relevance of the Gospel in shaping not only individual lives but also the communal and political structures of our time.

Artistic Expressions of Justice and Peace In the realm of Catholic imagination, where faith and creativity intertwine to create a tapestry of divine expressions, the thematic duo of justice and peace stand as towering pillars. These virtues, deeply embedded in the heart of Catholic social teaching, have found profound representations through various art forms across centuries. Artists, fueled by their faith and a fervent desire for a world that mirrors the Kingdom of Heaven, have harnessed their talents to champion the cause of the downtrodden and to herald an era of peace.

Historically, the Catholic Church has played a pivotal role in nurturing and patronizing artists who sought to explore themes of justice and peace. From the frescoes that adorn the walls of ancient basilicas to the somber melodies of sacred music, each form of art has carried within it the seeds of divine truth, aiming to awaken the conscience of the faithful and kindle a God-given desire for equity and harmony among men. This is not a mere artistic endeavor; it is a participation in the redemptive mission of Christ, who came "to bring good news to the poor...and to proclaim release to the captives" (Luke 4:18).

Consider the grand cathedrals of Europe, wherein the stained glass windows and soaring arches speak of a justice that elevates the soul towards divine realities. These sacred spaces, through their architectural magnificence, remind the faithful of the eternal justice of God, which surpasses the transient injustices of this world. In the silence of these holy edifices, one finds a peace that the world cannot give, a peace that flows from the assurance of God's unfailing justice.

In the realm of painting, artists such as Caravaggio have masterfully depicted biblical narratives that foreground themes of justice and redemption. His work, "The Calling of Saint Matthew," for example, illustrates the transformative power of divine mercy, inviting sinners to a new life of grace. This masterpiece, like many others, serves as a visual sermon, proclaiming the boundless mercy of God and His desire to restore justice through forgiveness and peace.

Music, with its ethereal beauty, has always been a powerful medium through which composers have explored and expressed the virtues of justice and peace. Gregorian chant, with its solemn and meditative qualities, transports the listener to a state of contemplation, where one can reflect on the profound truths of divine justice and the peace it engenders. Composers such as Palestrina and Mozart, in their sacred compositions, have encapsulated the prayers of the faithful, ascending like incense to the throne of God, supplicating for a world where justice and peace reign supreme.

Literature, too, has been an influential vessel for articulating Catholic teachings on justice and peace. Dante's "Divine Comedy," for instance, can be viewed as an epic journey towards divine justice, guiding the reader through the consequences of sin and the merciful restoration of order. Through allegory and sublime poetry, Dante invites readers to reflect on their own moral standings and the peace that comes from aligning one's life with divine will.

In the modern era, cinema and media have emerged as potent platforms for exploring the intricacies of justice and peace. Films directed by individuals of faith often grapple with these themes, challenging audiences to confront societal injustices and to advocate for a peaceful and just world. These stories, rooted in Gospel values, serve as modern parables, illustrating the enduring relevance of Christ's teachings in addressing contemporary issues.

Similarly, the digital landscape has become a fertile ground for Catholic artists to sow seeds of justice and peace. Through virtual art, blogs, and social media, artists can reach a global audience, spreading messages of hope, reconciliation, and divine justice. This digital evangelization, a sign of the times, harnesses the universal language of beauty to transcend cultural and geographical barriers.

It is essential to acknowledge that the pursuit of justice and peace through art is not without its challenges. Artists often face censorship, criticism, or indifference from those who view their expressions as confrontational or provocative. Yet, it is precisely in the face of such opposition that the role of the artist as a prophet comes to the fore. Courageously proclaiming the truth through their art, these creative individuals stand as beacons of hope, illuminating the path toward a just and peaceful society.

The Church, recognizing the invaluable contribution of artists in the mission of evangelization, calls upon the faithful to support and encourage artistic endeavors aimed at fostering justice and peace. This mutual collaboration between the Church and artists reflects the profound understanding that beauty, in its purest form, serves as a conduit for grace, drawing souls closer to God and to one another in a bond of solidarity.

In conclusion, the artistic expressions of justice and peace within the Catholic tradition are manifold and diverse. Each work of art, in its unique way, participates in the divine act of bringing about the Kingdom of God on earth. As stewards of God's creation and co-creators with Him, artists are entrusted with the noble task of weaving threads of justice and peace into the fabric of human culture. In doing so, they not only contribute to the beautification of the world but also facilitate the transformation of society according to the Gospel's vision of love and harmony.

The journey of integrating justice and peace into art is a continuous invitation to delve deeper into the mystery of God's love for humanity. Through their creative endeavors, artists echo the Creator's call to build a world where justice rolls down like waters, and peace like an ever-flowing stream (Amos 5:24). In this sacred mission, art and faith merge to reveal the splendor of God's vision for His creation, inviting all to partake in the banquet of divine justice and peace.

Chapter 11: Education and Formation through Beauty

In the rich tapestry that is Catholic education and formation, one thread stands out for its vivid color and texture: beauty. This is not beauty as it is often understood in a fleeting, superficial sense, but rather a profound form of beauty that lifts the soul towards the divine, guiding it in its earthly journey towards eternal salvation. This chapter delves into the indispensable role that art plays in Catholic education, showing how beauty serves as a powerful path to God.

Historically, the Church has always recognized the formative power of beauty. Its cathedrals, paintings, music, and literature are not merely artifacts of cultural heritage; they are instruments of evangelization and catechesis. Through them, the truths of the faith are made tangible, accessible, and, ultimately, irresistible. They speak to the human heart in a language beyond words, inviting it into a deeper encounter with the divine.

At the heart of Catholic pedagogy lies the principle that all creation reflects the beauty of its Creator. Thus, the study and creation of art within a Catholic framework is not a mere academic exercise but a form of worship, a way of engaging with the world as God's masterpiece. It's an approach to education that respects the whole person, recognizing the need for intellectual, emotional, and spiritual nourishment.

Beauty in Catholic education is not an optional extra; it's foundational. It cultivates the soil of the soul, preparing it to receive the seeds of truth and allowing them to flourish. This process begins with wonder, that initial spark of curiosity and awe that natural beauty and human artistry can evoke. Wonder opens the door to inquiry, dialogue, and ultimately, a deeper understanding of and relationship with God.

Indeed, the role of the arts in Catholic education extends beyond the classroom. Liturgical music, sacred architecture, and visual arts serve a catechetical function within the context of Mass and other liturgical celebrations. They are not mere adornments but essential expressions of faith, each element designed to draw participants deeper into the mystery of Christ.

The concept of beauty as a path to God is deeply scriptural. The Psalms, for instance, are filled with invitations to behold the beauty of the Lord and to worship Him in the splendor of holiness. This biblical understanding of beauty as a means of encountering God underpins the Church's use of art in education and formation.

In practical terms, integrating beauty into Catholic education involves more than just teaching the history of Christian art or music. It involves creating spaces that reflect beauty's transcendental qualities—truth, goodness, and beauty—thus providing an environment where students can encounter God. It means encouraging creativity and artistic expression as a vital aspect of human development and a powerful form of prayer and meditation.

Moreover, art can serve as a bridge across cultural and religious divides, offering a universal language that speaks to the human condition. In a diverse and often divided world, Catholic education can use beauty to promote understanding, compassion, and peace, illustrating the Church's mission to be a sign of unity in the midst of diversity.

In the face of modern challenges—where nihilism, relativism, and a culture of disposability often diminish the appreciation for beauty—the Church's commitment to education through beauty becomes all the more critical. It stands as a beacon of hope, a reminder of the dignity of the human person and the ultimate purpose of our existence.

Indeed, educators and formators who harness the power of beauty find themselves equipped with a potent tool for evangelization and catechesis. By leading students to encounter beauty in its truest form, they can open hearts to the beauty of the Gospel, which in turn can transform lives.

This transformative power of beauty is perhaps most evident in the lives of the saints, many of whom were profoundly moved by their encounters with beauty, whether through nature, art, or the liturgy. These encounters often led to deep conversions, illustrating beauty's capacity to draw the soul toward God and to inspire a life of holiness.

Therefore, it becomes clear that education and formation within the Catholic tradition cannot be complete without a robust engagement with beauty. By reclaiming beauty's rightful place in Catholic education, the Church can offer the world a vision of hope and redemption, grounded in the recognition of all creation as a reflection of the Creator's beauty.

Ultimately, education and formation through beauty are about more than aesthetics; they are about recognizing the sacramental nature of the world and our call to co-create with God. In this way, art becomes a form of prayer, a means of sanctification, and a path to deeper union with the divine.

In conclusion, as the Church faces the challenges of the 21st century, the need for beauty in education and formation has never been greater. By fostering environments where beauty is celebrated and cherished, the Church can continue to draw souls to Christ, using art as a vehicle for evangelization, catechesis, and ultimately, salvation.

The Role of Art in Catholic Education

The integration of art within the framework of Catholic education is not merely an additive feature; it's a foundational aspect, deeply rooted in the Church's understanding of beauty as a pathway to the Divine. This integration is crucial in shaping individuals who are not only intellectually adept but also spiritually enriched, capable of appreciating the profound relationship between the earthly and the heavenly.

At the heart of Catholic education, there exists a profound recognition that beauty does more than please the senses; it elevates the soul, enabling a deeper communion with God. Through art, students encounter an aesthetic experience that transcends the mundane, pointing towards the ineffable mystery of the Almighty. This education isn't confined to the dissemination of knowledge; it's an invitation to a journey of discovery, where beauty acts as both the guide and the destination.

In this vibrant tapestry of learning, art serves as a vital thread, weaving together the material and the spiritual, the human and the divine. It fosters an environment where students are encouraged to explore their creative talents as gifts from God, meant to be nurtured and offered back in service to Him and to humanity. This nurturing goes beyond mere technical skill; it involves cultivating an artistic sensibility that sees the hand of God in all creation and seeks to replicate that divine creativity in human form.

Historically, the Catholic Church has been a patron of the arts, understanding their value in expressing spiritual truths and enhancing worship. This legacy of patronage is mirrored within Catholic education, where art is not peripheral but central to the curriculum. It reinforces the Church's mission of evangelization, providing students with a language that can bridge cultures and reach hearts in a way words alone cannot.

Art education within this context is inherently sacramental, embodying an outward sign of inward grace. It recognizes the artist's role as a co-creator with God, emphasizing the responsibility to create works that uphold the good, the true, and the beautiful. This sacramental view shapes how art is both taught and perceived, encouraging students to approach their creative endeavors with reverence for the divine origin of their talents.

The pedagogical approaches in Catholic art education are therefore distinct, aiming not just at developing technical proficiency but at forming the whole person. This formation includes an aesthetic literacy that enables students to critically engage with the world's beauty and, in doing so, discern the presence of God. It cultivates an appreciation for the sacred, fostering a realization that beauty, in its purest essence, is a reflection of the Divine Beauty.

Moreover, Catholic art education extends beyond the classroom, permeating the entire educational environment. From the architecture of the school buildings to the selection of art displayed within them, every element is intended to educate, to elevate the mind and spirit towards God. It's an education that speaks silently but powerfully through every line, color, and form encountered by the students.

This holistic approach to education through beauty is transformative, enabling students to become not just consumers of art but patrons and creators, equipped to contribute to the cultural landscape with works that reflect their faith. It inspires a sense of mission, urging them to employ their talents in service to the Church and the world, seeking to beautify the temporal with glimpses of the eternal.

Inclusivity is another hallmark of Catholic art education, which embraces a wide array of artistic expressions from different cultures and epochs. This diversity reflects the catholicity of the Church itself and offers students a richer palette from which to draw inspiration. It teaches them that the quest for beauty transcends cultural and historical boundaries, uniting humanity in a common yearning for the divine.

Furthermore, Catholic art education places a strong emphasis on the moral dimensions of art, prompting students to consider the ethical implications of their creative choices. It questions the notion of art for art's sake and replaces it with a vision of art for God's sake. In this way, it contributes to the moral formation of the students, equipping them to make choices that are not only aesthetically pleasing but also morally sound and spiritually uplifting.

The challenges facing Catholic art education in the contemporary world are manifold, ranging from the commodification of art to the pervasive influence of secularism. However, these challenges only underscore the importance of this educational mission. In a culture often devoid of meaning and beauty, Catholic art education stands as a beacon of hope, affirming the enduring power of beauty to convey truth and to transform hearts.

Consequently, the role of art in Catholic education is indispensable. It's an education that shapes visionaries, capable of seeing beyond the visible to the eternal truths it signifies. It forms individuals who are not only knowledgeable about the arts but are also imbued with a sense of their vocation to be stewards of beauty in the world.

In conclusion, the integration of art in Catholic education is a powerful testament to the Church's conviction that beauty is a vital pathway to God. It embodies a holistic approach to learning, where students are invited to engage with the world aesthetically and spiritually. Through this engagement, they are prepared to fulfill their role as bearers of beauty, contributing to the sanctification of the world and the glorification of God.

The endeavor to educate through beauty, then, is not merely an educational strategy but a profound engagement with the sacred, an act of faith in the power of beauty to reveal the face of God to humanity.

Beauty as a Path to God

In the preceding discourse of Catholic thought and culture, it is evident that the richness of Catholic tradition encompasses a vast array of expressions, through which the divine is made tangible. It is within this continuity of exploration and expression that the concept of beauty, particularly as a pathway to God, emerges not as an ancillary notion but as a central strand of Catholic heritage. This section delves into the intrinsic relationship between beauty and divinity, positing that beauty serves not merely as an aesthetic indulgence but as a beacon leading to the transcendent and ultimately, to God Himself.

The idea of beauty as a path to God is rooted deeply in the notion that all creation reflects the beauty of its Creator. Thus, to encounter beauty, whether it is manifested in art, nature, or human interactions, is to catch a glimpse of the divine spark from which all creation has emerged. In Catholic thought, beauty is synonymous with truth and goodness – a trinity of ideals that converge to reflect the ultimate truth and beauty found in God. This unity of truth, beauty, and goodness forms a pathway by which the human heart is drawn to seek what is beyond the material.

Art, as a quintessential manifestation of beauty, holds a pivotal role in this spiritual journey. Catholic art, with its rich tradition spanning across centuries, serves as a profound medium through which the divine mysteries are made accessible to humanity. Through art, the abstract aspects of faith are translated into tangible forms, inviting an encounter with the divine that transcends the limitations of language and intellect. The role of the artist, therefore, is imbued with a sacred purpose – to bridge the gap between the divine and the human, enabling an encounter with God through the medium of beauty.

Historically, the Catholic Church has recognized the immense capacity of beauty to convey the sacred. From the architectural grandeur of cathedrals to the reverent devotion captured in religious icons, art has been employed as a vehicle for worship and contemplation. In these sacred spaces and images, beauty serves as a conduit for divine grace, nurturing the soul's longing for God. This integration of beauty into worship underscores the belief that beauty is not solely for edification but is itself a form of prayer.

However, the path of beauty to God is not confined to religious art but extends to the natural world. The splendor of creation reflects the masterful artistry of God, revealing signs of His presence in the world. The Catholic tradition encourages a sacramental view of the world, where material elements of creation are seen as bearers of grace. In this light, beauty becomes a sacrament of sorts, a visible sign of an invisible grace, drawing those who encounter it into a deeper communion with the Creator.

A pivotal aspect of this journey is the cultivation of a discerning eye, one that perceives the inherent beauty in the world as a reflection of divine beauty. This requires a contemplative posture, a willingness to see beyond the surface and recognize the sacramentality of creation. The pursuit of beauty, then, is not merely an aesthetic endeavor but a spiritual discipline that nurtures the soul's capacity to perceive and respond to the divine presence in all things.

The implications of beauty as a path to God extend into the moral and ethical dimensions of life. In a world marred by brokenness and despair, beauty has the power to restore hope and illuminate the goodness that persists amid suffering. Through art and creation, beauty testifies to the possibility of redemption, pointing towards the transformative power of God's grace. It challenges the prevailing narrative of nihilism and despair, offering instead a vision of the world that affirms the inherent worth and dignity of creation.

In the educational sphere, the integration of beauty into learning experiences becomes a means of forming individuals who not only appreciate the aesthetic dimensions of life but who are also attuned to the moral and spiritual values reflected in beauty. By fostering an appreciation for beauty, Catholic education cultivates a holistic view of the human person, one that honors the intrinsic connection between the aesthetic, moral, and spiritual dimensions of life.

Within the ecclesial community, beauty serves as a unifying force, transcending cultural and linguistic barriers to create a shared experience of the sacred. The universal appeal of beauty facilitates a sense of communion among the faithful, fostering a collective identity rooted in a common aspiration towards the divine. Through liturgical celebrations, religious art, and sacred music, the community of believers is invited to partake in a foretaste of the heavenly banquet, where beauty and truth coalesce in the beatific vision of God.

As the world continues to evolve, with new forms of art and expression emerging, the path of beauty to God remains ever relevant. The challenge for the contemporary Catholic artist is to discern and articulate the presence of the divine in the midst of a rapidly changing cultural landscape. In doing so, the artist participates in the ongoing creation of the world, cooperating with God's grace to reveal the beauty that leads to Him.

In conclusion, the understanding of beauty as a path to God offers a rich and multifaceted perspective on the role of art and creation in the spiritual life. It affirms that beauty, in its myriad manifestations, is not an end in itself but a means by which the human heart is drawn towards the ultimate Beauty, who is God. Through the cultivation of a sacramental vision of the world, individuals are invited to embark on a journey of discovery, where every encounter with beauty becomes an opportunity for encountering the divine.

Chapter 12: Mission and Evangelization: Reaching Out through Art

As we forge ahead into the heart of our exploration of Catholic art, we come to understand its pivotal role in mission and evangelization. Art, in its most divine form, serves as a bridge between Heaven and Earth, enabling a dialogue that transcends words and enters the realm of the soul. In this chapter, we delve into the ways in which art becomes not just a vehicle for personal expression, but a universal language through which the Church reaches out to the world, beckoning all towards the truth, goodness, and beauty of God.

At the core of Catholic teaching is the principle that beauty is a path to God. This idea, deeply embedded within our tradition, posits that art has the capacity to reveal aspects of God's nature and to evoke a response of love and desire for the divine. From the intricate designs of ancient cathedrals to the profound simplicity of sacred music, every artistic creation reflects a facet of the infinite beauty of the Creator, drawing souls closer to the mystery of God's love.

The principle of 'ars sacra,' or sacred art, has long held that true art does more than appeal to the senses—it evangelizes, speaks to the heart, and converts the soul. Through the ages, artists have been custodians of this sacred duty, channeling their God-given talents into works that transcend cultural and linguistic barriers. In doing so, they engage in the New Evangelization, a mission aimed at rekindling faith in regions where Christianity has become culturally stagnant.

The universality of art makes it an ideal medium for evangelization. In a world steeped in visual culture, the power of an image to convey complex theological truths or to inspire a movement towards conversion cannot be underestimated. It's in the silent contemplation of Michelangelo's Pietà, for instance, that many find a profound understanding of Christ's sacrifice and Mary's sorrow, opening the heart to the mystery of redemptive suffering.

Furthermore, contemporary challenges call for a reimagining of ways to evangelize. In an era of digital immediacy and fleeting attention spans, the timeless beauty of sacred art offers a counterbalance, inviting a deeper, meditative engagement with the divine. This is not merely about absorbing an image; it's about allowing it to penetrate our hearts and transform our understanding of God's presence in our lives.

Art also serves as a form of catechesis, teaching the faith where words alone may fail. Through the portrayal of biblical scenes, the lives of the saints, and the depiction of Christ's Parables, artists unpack the mysteries of the faith, making them accessible and engaging to all, irrespective of their level of theological education.

The call to evangelize through art is not limited to the artistically gifted few; it is a universal call to every member of the faithful. By supporting the arts within the Church and fostering an environment where beauty is recognized and cherished, we all partake in the mission of evangelization. This nurturing of beauty within our churches, homes, and communities serves as a beacon of light in a world often darkened by despair and unbelief.

The New Evangelization urges us to utilize art in evangelization with renewed vigor, recognizing its potential to reach souls in a deeply personal way. It's through beauty that one's heart can be opened to the truths of the Gospel, making art a silent yet powerful preacher of the faith.

Moreover, the inculturation of the Gospel through art ensures that its message resonates across different cultures and societies. By embracing local artistic traditions and integrating them with the universality of the Catholic faith, the Church speaks a language that is both native and universal, engaging people in their own cultural context.

As we look to the future, the role of artists within the Church must be both cherished and challenged. Artists are called not just to create, but to pray through their creation, seeking to imbue every work with the light of Christ. It is here, in the confluence of divine inspiration and human creativity, that art becomes a true act of worship and a tool for evangelization.

In conclusion, the mission to evangelize through art is both ancient and ever-new. As the Church moves forward, it must continue to embrace the arts, recognizing in them the power to touch hearts, change lives, and draw souls closer to God. Through a renewed commitment to the beauty of sacred art, we participate in the ongoing work of salvation, using every brushstroke, note, and word to spread the Gospel to the ends of the earth.

Let us then, as a community of believers, recommit ourselves to this noble mission. May our churches, homes, and hearts become galleries of divine beauty, where every creation speaks of God's love and invites all to encounter Him. The mission field of art is vast, and the harvest is indeed plentiful. With creativity and faith as our guides, let us go forth, reaching out through art to evangelize the world.

The New Evangelization and Culture

In the unfolding tapestry of the Church's mission, the call to a New Evangelization emerges as a clarion reminder of our collective calling to reap the harvest of faith in contemporary society. This calling, deeply rooted in the fertile ground of culture, finds in art an unparalleled medium of expression and dialogue. Art serves not merely as a reflection of the divine but as an active participant in the sacred mission of evangelization, engaging cultures and transforming them from within.

At the heart of this evangelistic thrust is the recognition of culture as a living, breathing entity, constantly evolving yet perennially seeking truth, beauty, and goodness. The Church, in her wisdom, understands that to engage culture effectively, she must speak its language. Art becomes this lingua franca, transcending linguistic and geographical boundaries, touching hearts, and elevating minds to the contemplation of the divine mystery.

The New Evangelization calls for a rekindling of the Christian message, emphasizing not only its timelessness but also its relevance in today's world. This rekindling is not a mere repetition of what has been but a creative engagement with the present moment, leveraging the full spectrum of human creativity to illuminate the face of Christ to a world in flux. Artists, endowed with the unique ability to see the world through the lens of beauty, become crucial laborers in this vineyard, crafting works that resonate with the contemporary human experience while drawing from the eternal wellspring of faith.

This synergy between evangelization and culture, mediated through art, is not without its challenges. A culture that often prizes the novel over the true, and the immediate over the eternal, can be a hostile terrain for the seeds of the Gospel. Yet, it is precisely in this space that Catholic artists are called to labor, to bridge the gap between the sacred and the secular, inviting an encounter with the transcendent through the beauty and profundity of their work.

The Church's call to utilize art in the service of the New Evangelization is not a call to instrumentalize art but to recognize its intrinsic power to communicate the divine. As St. John Paul II eloquently articulated in his Letter to Artists (1999), artists are "custodians of beauty," called to make visible the invisible, to reveal the face of God through their creative endeavors. This sacred duty, rooted in the co-creative partnership between the artist and the divine, elevates art from mere decoration to a form of prayer and proclamation.

In this vein, the New Evangelization and culture converge in a dynamic interplay of faith and artistry. Through the universal language of art, the Church speaks to every heart, inviting all to encounter the beauty that saves. It is in this encounter that barriers fall, hearts are opened, and the Gospel finds fertile ground in which to take root and flourish.

Thus, the mission of evangelization through art is both a privilege and a responsibility for Catholic artists. In their hands lies the potential to weave a new narrative of faith, one that resonates with the signs of the times while anchored firmly in the timeless truth of the Gospel. By embracing this mission, artists participate in the Church's perennial task of bringing Christ to the world and the world to Christ.

In conclusion, the New Evangelization and culture, manifested through the medium of art, offer a beacon of hope and a bridge to the divine in a world often marred by fragmentation and disillusionment. Through their talents, artists are endowed with the noble task of illuminating the beauty of the Gospel, crafting works that not only speak to the mind and heart but also invite the soul to ascend to the heights of divine contemplation.

As the Church continues to navigate the complexities of the modern world, the integration of faith, culture, and art remains a vital pathway to engaging and evangelizing the culture of our time. In this grand mission, every stroke of the brush, every note of music, and every crafted word becomes a testament to the enduring power of beauty to convey truth and inspire a deeper communion with the Creator.

Art as a Universal Language No other form of communication transcends the boundaries of time, culture, and personal experience as profoundly as art does. In the Catholic tradition, art holds a distinguished place, serving not only as a medium for aesthetic expression but also as a vital tool for education, conversion, and delivering the message of divine grace. This narrative seeks to explore the universal language of art, emphasizing its capability to resonate across diverse landscapes of thought and spirituality, and highlighting its role in the grand tapestry of Catholic evangelization.

The concept of art as a universal language is deeply entrenched in the Catholic imagination, which views artistic creation as a mirror reflecting the eternal beauty and truth of God. From the intricate designs of Gothic cathedrals to the tranquil beauty of Gregorian chants, each artistic endeavor aims to speak directly to the soul, transcending linguistic and cultural barriers. This is because art, in its essence, communicates through symbols, emotions, and experiences that are fundamentally human, making it accessible to all, regardless of their background or beliefs.

In the realm of Catholic thought, the universality of art is not just theoretical but practical. The Church has historically employed art as a catechetical tool, reaching out to those who could not read or did not have access to sacred texts. The stained glass windows of medieval churches, for example, served as visual bibles, narrating biblical stories and the lives of saints to the congregations. Such manifestations of art speak volumes about its capacity to educate and inspire faith among diverse audiences.

Moreover, art serves as a bridge between the divine and the human, offering glimpses of the transcendent through the material world. The beauty inherent in Catholic art points to a beauty beyond itself, leading the soul on a journey towards the Ultimate Beauty, which is God. By engaging with art, individuals embark on a path of spiritual contemplation and discovery, regardless of their initial intentions or beliefs.

Central to the universal language of art is its power to evoke a shared human experience. Whether it's the agony captured in Michelangelo's Pieta or the serene devotion in a painting of the Madonna and Child, Catholic art often encapsulates the range of human emotions, from suffering to joy, in a way that is universally relatable. This shared emotional landscape enables art to connect deeply with individuals from all walks of life, fostering empathy, understanding, and, ultimately, a sense of unity.

Art also plays a pivotal role in the process of conversion and spiritual renewal. The beauty and profundity of a piece of art can stir the soul, prompting reflection, questioning, and, in some cases, a profound reorientation of one's life towards God. The stories of individuals encountering God through art are numerous and speak to art's powerful ability to touch hearts and minds in unexpected ways.

The universality of art is further reflected in its ability to adapt and evolve with cultural contexts. While the core messages of faith, hope, and love remain constant, their artistic expressions are fluid, taking on new forms and styles that resonate with different age groups and cultures. This adaptability ensures that art remains a relevant and compelling medium for evangelization in every era.

Education and formation through beauty, as envisioned in the Catholic tradition, inherently rely on the universality of art. By engaging with art, individuals not only appreciate its aesthetic value but also deepen their understanding of theological truths and moral teachings. The transformative power of sacred music, the storytelling capacity of religious plays, and the visual splendor of liturgical arts all contribute to a holistic educational experience that appeals to the intellect and the senses alike.

In contemporary society, where communication is increasingly visual and digital, the universal language of art has taken on new significance. Catholic artists and creators are finding innovative ways to use virtual art, film, and media to tell the story of faith in ways that speak to the modern heart and mind. In this digital age, art continues to serve as a vital means for the Church to reach out, communicate, and connect with wider audiences.

Art as a universal language is not just about the transmission of religious ideals; it's also about fostering a dialogue—a conversation between the divine and the human, the sacred and the secular. This dialogue is essential in today's pluralistic society, where understanding and respecting differences are paramount. Through art, the Catholic Church invites everyone into a conversation, not to erase distinctions, but to find common ground and shared beauty.

Understanding art as a universal language also challenges artists and consumers of art alike to approach art with intentionality and reverence. Knowing that art has the power to transcend and transform, individuals are called to engage with it in a way that is open, reflective, and seeking deeper truth. This thoughtful engagement with art fosters a culture that values beauty, seeks understanding, and aspires towards the transcendent.

In the Catholic ethos, the ultimate goal of art is not merely aesthetic pleasure but the glorification of God and the sanctification of the viewer. Thus, art serves a dual purpose: it is both an offering to God and a means of grace for humanity. By participating in the universal language of art, individuals participate in the ongoing creation and revelation of God's beauty in the world.

In conclusion, the universality of art is a testament to its enduring power and relevance in the Catholic tradition and beyond. As a language that speaks to the deepest truths of human existence, art has the unique capacity to unite, educate, and inspire. It stands as a luminous beacon of faith, calling all who encounter it towards the divine, towards beauty, and towards a greater understanding of themselves and each other.

Looking towards the future, the Church continues to embrace the universal language of art as a means of evangelization, education, and encounter. In a world that is often divided, art remains a powerful symbol of hope, a reminder that beyond our differences, there exists a Beauty that can bring us together, elevating our spirits and drawing us closer to the divine.

Chapter 13: Sacred Spaces: Architecture and Liturgy

In the heart of Catholic worship and community life lies a profound encounter with the divine, an encounter facilitated not only through the holy sacraments and liturgical rites but also through the very spaces in which these sacred activities unfold. The architecture of Catholic churches is not merely a backdrop for spiritual events; it is, in essence, a participant, a silent preacher of the Gospels, designed to elevate the mind and soul towards the contemplation of God and His mysteries. The language of Catholic architecture, with its lofty spires, massive domes, and intricate stained glass, speaks volumes about the faith's understanding of the sacred, creating spaces for an encounter with God that is both intimate and awe-inspiring.

At the core of Catholic architectural design is the Liturgy itself, a divine drama that unfolds through the Eucharist and the sacraments within these sacred spaces. Architects throughout history have been tasked with translating theological concepts and liturgical requirements into concrete and stone, giving rise to structures that not only accommodate but also enhance the liturgical actions taking place within. This intricate dance between form and function, between space and spirit, is what characterizes Catholic churches, transforming them from mere buildings into gateways to the divine.

The development of church architecture has been influenced by numerous styles over the centuries, from the solemn grandeur of Romanesque to the celestial heights of Gothic, the reflective simplicity of baroque, and beyond. Each era's architecture reflects a particular theological emphasis, an evolving understanding of God's relationship with humanity. For instance, Gothic cathedrals, with their pointed arches and ribbed vaults, invite the eye and spirit upward, symbolizing the soul's ascent to God, whereas Romanesque architecture, with its heavy, earthbound elements, emphasizes God's immanence and the mystery of the incarnation (Macaulay, 1953).

However, the true essence of Catholic architecture transcends these stylistic differences, rooted in the sacramentality that underpins the Catholic faith. This sacramentality recognizes the material world as a channel of divine grace, a belief that is manifested in the careful and deliberate use of materials, light, and space in church buildings. The design of a church is meant to reflect the heavenly Jerusalem, a foretaste of the eternal, making palpable the unseen realities of faith. The layout, the orientation towards the east, the allocation of sacred spaces within the church, all serve to orient the faithful towards the ultimate sacred space: the Kingdom of God (Schoenauer, 1981).

In conclusion, the architecture of Catholic churches represents a profound intermingling of art, theology, and liturgy. Through centuries, architects and church builders have endeavored to create spaces that not only serve the practical needs of worship but also tell the story of faith, a story of a God who became man and dwelt among us. As sacred spaces, these churches stand as a testament to the enduring presence of the divine in the world, inviting all who enter to pause, reflect, and encounter God in a profound and transformative way.

The Language of Catholic Architecture

In delving into the language of Catholic architecture, we embark on an exploration of the sacred spaces that facilitate an encounter with the Divine. Architecture, in its most profound sense, serves not just as a shelter or abode, but as a lexicon of faith, a tangible manifestation of the ineffable. It stands as an edifice of belief, narrating the stories of salvation, sanctity, and the sacramental life through its very structure.

The foundational elements of Catholic architecture are deeply rooted in the historical unfolding of the Church's journey through the ages. Each architectural feature speaks to a theological truth, guiding the faithful closer to the mysteries of the faith they profess. The nave, the transepts, the altar—each of these elements serves a specific liturgical function, yes, but they also communicate far deeper spiritual realities.

The nave, often teeming with the congregation, symbolizes the Church Militant—the faithful on their earthly pilgrimage. Its very orientation towards the altar draws our gaze and steps forward, mirroring the soul's journey toward God. This spatial arrangement does not merely facilitate the gathering of people; it embodies the communal march towards salvation. The architectural design thus becomes a catechesis, a silent teacher of faith.

Transcending the nave, the altar stands as the central locus of Catholic worship. It is more than a table for sacrifice; it is Christ himself, the living stone (1 Peter 2:4). In the design and placement of the altar, Catholic architecture communicates the sacrificial heart of the faith, encapsulating the mystery of the Eucharist. Thus, the altar is often elevated, adorned, and centrally located, drawing all attention and action towards the Paschal Mystery made present at each Mass.

The grandeur of Catholic cathedrals, with their soaring spires and stunning stained glass, is not merely for aesthetic delight. These elements serve a sacramental purpose, using beauty to lift the heart and mind to God. The vertical lines of Gothic architecture, for example, guide the eye heavenward, symbolizing the soul's aspiration towards the divine. Meanwhile, stained glass windows narrate the scriptural stories or saintly lives, illuminating the interior with a divine light that teaches and transforms.

Light in Catholic architecture carries profound symbolism. The play of natural light through stained glass windows not only creates an atmosphere of reverence and wonder but also represents the illuminating presence of God's grace in our lives. As sunlight changes throughout the day, so too does the portrayal of these holy images, reminding us of the dynamic presence of the Holy Spirit, ever active and moving within the sacred space.

The architectural silence of monastic cloisters speaks volumes of the contemplative aspect of the faith. These enclosed courtyards, with their arcades and central gardens, offer a serene tableau for prayer and reflection, embodying the call to interiority and communion with God. They mirror the cloistered chambers of our hearts, spaces set apart for divine encounter.

Baptisteries and confessionals, though distinct, speak to the theme of conversion and renewal within the Church's architectural language. Through their design and placement, these spaces signify the ongoing journey of repentance and rebirth that characterizes the Christian life. Baptisteries often feature intricate designs and symbols of death and resurrection, emphasizing baptism as a sacramental entrance into new life in Christ.

In the confessionals, the architecture underscores the intimacy and privacy necessary for the sacrament of reconciliation. Small, enclosed, and often dimly lit, these spaces facilitate a personal encounter with God's mercy, away from the public gaze. Their design reflects the theology of reconciliation—encouraging humility, facilitating confession, and ensuring the discrete and sacred handling of penitence.

The grand facades of many Catholic churches are not just decorative fronts but catechetical statements in stone. They are often adorned with sculptures of saints, biblical scenes, and theological symbols, serving as a visual proclamation of the faith to the external world.

These facades invite the faithful and curious alike into the mysteries contained within, serving both as an evangelistic call and a testament to the Church's enduring presence through time.

Beyond the structural elements, the very materials used in Catholic architecture speak of the incarnation of faith. The use of wood, stone, metal, and glass carries with them symbolic meanings—wood reminding us of the cross, stone of the church's firm foundation, metal of strength and durability, and glass of transparency and the play of divine light. Every material choice articulates aspects of the theological and spiritual journey.

The integration of art into architecture further intensifies the language of Catholic spaces. Iconography in the Eastern rite, statuary in the West, and the universal use of altarpieces and murals create a visual theology. These artistic elements function as scripture for the illiterate and a source of meditative contemplation for all, enriching the liturgical experience and deepening the encounter with the sacred.

The architectural design of Catholic spaces also reflects the universality of the Church. From the grandeur of European cathedrals to the modesty of mission churches in the developing world, the diversity of styles and expressions reveals the catholicity—the universality and inclusivity—of the faith. It speaks to a Church that transcends culture, time, and place, yet is incarnationally present in the local community.

Ultimately, the language of Catholic architecture serves to create spaces for encounter with God. These sacred spaces are designed to lift the human spirit, to aid in the worship of the divine, and to facilitate the sacramental life. Through its structures and symbols, Catholic architecture speaks of a faith that is both ancient and ever new, inviting all to come and see, to experience the presence of the living God.

In the silent stones, the lofty domes, the light-drenched naves, and the intimate chapels, Catholic architecture reveals its profound language—a language of beauty, mystery, and divine presence, calling the faithful to worship and the world to wonder.

Creating Spaces for Encounter with God Within the vast expanse of Catholic tradition, architecture serves not merely as a shelter for the faithful but as a profound expression of faith itself. This chapter delves into the sacred act of creating spaces that transcend their physical boundaries to become places where heaven and earth meet, where the divine presence is felt, and where the soul encounters God in a profound and transformative way.

At the heart of Catholic architecture lies the principle that beauty acts as a conduit to the divine. This belief roots itself in the notion that God, the ultimate Creator, has imbued creation with beauty, order, and harmony. Thus, when architects and artists engage in the creation of liturgical spaces, they participate in a divine act, mirroring the Creator's work by making visible the invisible realm of the spiritual.

The design of these sacred spaces takes into account not only aesthetic considerations but also the theological and liturgical requirements of the Catholic faith. This demands a deep understanding of the Church's rites, symbols, and sacramental theology. Liturgical spaces are designed to facilitate the sacraments, especially the Eucharist, making their layout and ornamentation integral to the liturgical experience.

Historically, the architecture of Catholic churches has evolved to meet the needs of the faithful while reflecting the theological and artistic sensibilities of the time. From the grandiose basilicas of ancient Rome to the soaring Gothic cathedrals of medieval Europe, each style serves the same purpose: to lift the human heart to God. These buildings, with their vast spaces, intricate iconography, and play of light and shadow, are designed to evoke awe, wonder, and a sense of the sacred.

The role of light in Catholic architecture cannot be overstated. It serves not just as a practical necessity but as a metaphor for Christ, the Light of the World. The thoughtful manipulation of natural light, especially in the design of windows and the orientation of buildings, is a key element in creating a sacred atmosphere, leading the faithful from darkness into the light of God's presence.

Moreover, the use of sacred art and iconography within these spaces acts as a form of visual theology. Frescoes, mosaics, statues, and stained glass tell the stories of the faith, instructing and inspiring the faithful. In this way, art and architecture work in concert to create an environment that educates, nurtures faith, and facilitates encounter with the divine.

In the design of modern sacred spaces, architects face the challenge of adhering to tradition while responding to contemporary needs and sensibilities. This often involves integrating modern materials and technologies without sacrificing the sense of transcendence and tradition. The successful modern church building respects the past, meets present needs, and opens to future possibilities, all the while leading the faithful closer to God.

The spatial configuration of a church—its nave, sanctuary, and altar—is laden with symbolic meaning, echoing the journey of the Christian life. The layout is carefully considered to reflect theological truths, such as the progression from the worldly to the divine, from sin to salvation. Sacred spaces guide the movement of the faithful, both physically and spiritually, toward God.

Sound also plays a crucial role in creating a space for encounter with God. Acoustics are designed to uplift the spoken word and sacred music, enhancing prayer and worship. The resonance of a church space can heighten the sense of the sacred and facilitate communal worship, allowing the beauty of choirs and congregational singing to elevate the soul.

Not to be overlooked is the importance of the aesthetic and functional aspects of church furniture, including altars, pulpits, and pews. These elements are crafted not only for their use but to harmonize with the sacred space, contributing to the overall spiritual experience. Through their beauty and craftsmanship, they too speak of the divine.

The creation of sacred spaces extends beyond churches to include chapels, shrines, and even outdoor spaces designed for contemplation and prayer. Each of these places, whether grand or humble, serves the purpose of facilitating an encounter with God. They are spaces where the faithful can gather to worship, reflect, and find peace in God's presence.

In conclusion, the art and architecture of Catholic sacred spaces embody a profound understanding of humanity's quest for God. They stand as testament to the Church's belief in the power of beauty to elevate the spirit and draw the faithful closer to the Divine. Through thoughtful design that integrates form, function, and symbolism, these spaces facilitate moments of profound encounter between God and His people.

As stewards of this sacred heritage, architects, artists, and the faithful are called to appreciate, preserve, and create spaces that not only meet the physical and aesthetic needs of the Church but also embody its deepest spiritual aspirations. In doing so, they participate in the ongoing story of salvation, contributing to the Church's mission of bringing God's presence into the world.

The design of sacred spaces is thus not only an art; it is a mission, a participation in the divine work of salvation. It is through these spaces that the Church continues to fulfill its calling to be a beacon of hope, a refuge for the soul, and a foretaste of the heavenly kingdom.

Chapter 14: Religious Orders and Artistic Legacy

The annals of history are vivid with the hues of divine artistry, a testament to the sacred interplay between faith and creativity. Within this sacred narrative, the religious orders of the Catholic Church stand as monumental pillars, each contributing uniquely to the edifice of Christian artistic heritage. In the following discourse, we traverse the vast landscapes of imagination and devotion, exploring how these religious communities have not only championed but also fundamentally shaped the trajectory of sacred art.

The Benedictines, known for their motto "Ora et Labora" (pray and work), have imbibed this ethos into every brushstroke and chisel mark they have bestowed upon the canvas of Christendom. Their monasteries emerged as cradles of preservation during tumultuous periods in history, safeguarding not just manuscripts but also the techniques and artistic wisdom of antiquity (Dreves & Blume, 1901). Architectural marvels, such as the Abbey of Saint Gall, stand as lasting testaments to the Benedictine's profound impact on religious and cultural landscapes.

The Franciscans, following the humble path laid by St. Francis of Assisi, embraced the beauty of creation in all its forms, disseminating a vision of beauty that was palpable in its simplicity and depth. Their contribution to the arts, particularly in the realms of painting and sculpture, reflect a profound reverence for nature and an intimate portrayal of Christ's humanity. The works of Giotto, though not a Franciscan himself, were deeply inspired by Franciscan spirituality, capturing the essence of divine love and compassion in a manner that resonated with the laity and clergy alike (Ladis, 1993).

The Dominicans, founded by St. Dominic, pursued truth through contemplation and scholarship. This intellectual fervor found its expression in the arts, most notably through the preaching of Fra Angelico, a Dominican friar whose works were sermons in themselves. His frescoes in the convent of San Marco in Florence are a testament to the Dominican dedication to using art as a vehicle for theological discourse, blending doctrinal precision with aesthetic sublimity.

The Society of Jesus, or Jesuits, founded by St. Ignatius of Loyola, espoused a pedagogy that intertwined the arts with the cultivation of virtue and religious devotion. The Jesuit contribution to the arts was characterized by a dramatic flair and an innovative engagement with the visual and performing arts as means of catechesis and spiritual enrichment. The baroque grandeur of Jesuit churches across Europe and Latin America serves as a vivid illustration of their approach to using art as a means of evoking spiritual awe and reflection (Bailey, 1999).

These religious orders, each with their distinctive charisms, have collectively woven a rich tapestry of artistic legacy that continues to inspire and edify. Their contributions underscore a sacred synergy between faith and art, revealing the manifold ways in which the divine can be encountered and expressed. In the continuous interplay of light and shadow, form and color, these orders have not only depicted the mysteries of faith but have also invited the faithful into a deeper participation in the divine mystery.

As we delve into the specifics of each order's artistic contributions, we discern not mere artifacts of a bygone era but living testimonies of faith in action. The Benedictines, with their architectural and literary achievements, remind us of the sanctity of work and prayer. The Franciscans, through their depictions of nature and humanity, teach us the beauty of humility and compassion. The Dominicans, with their doctrinal rigor expressed through art, call us to a deeper contemplation of truth. And the Jesuits, through their dramatic and educational pursuits, challenge us to engage the world and our faith with renewed zeal and creativity.

In examining this confluence of religious devotion and artistic expression, we are not merely spectators but are invited into a participatory relationship with the divine. Through the legacy of these religious orders, we are reminded that art, in its most sublime form, is a conduit of grace, a means through which we encounter the ineffable, and a path to transcendence.

As the epochs turn and humanity continues its relentless quest for beauty and meaning, the artistic heritage left by these orders serves as a beacon, illuminating the unending interplay between divine inspiration and human creativity. It is in this sacred space, where heaven and earth converge, that the arts offer a glimpse into the eternal, beckoning us to look beyond the veil and witness the glory of the Creator reflected in the beauty of creation.

Thus, the legacy of religious orders in the realm of art is not confined to the annals of history or the walls of museums and churches. It is a living legacy that continues to inspire, challenge, and transform, inviting all who encounter it to embark on a journey of faith, beauty, and contemplation.

In concluding this reflection on the artistic legacy of religious orders, one cannot help but marvel at the profound ways in which creativity, fueled by devout faith, has served as a bridge between the human and the divine. In the multitude of forms and expressions, the sacred artistry of these communities continues to bear witness to the enduring power of beauty as a vehicle of divine revelation and human transformation.

In the spirit of these great traditions, may we too seek to engage the arts as a sacred offering, a testament to the beauty of the divine, and a means through which the grace of God continues to illuminate the depths of the human soul.

The Benedictine Contribution to Art and Culture

In the grand tapestry of Catholic art and culture, the thread woven by the Benedictine Order is both deep and luminous. Founded by St. Benedict of Nursia in the 6th century, the Order has left an indelible mark on the development and propagation of Christian art and thought. This legacy, rooted in the principle of 'Ora et Labora' (pray and work), encapsulates the Benedictine ethos of uniting spiritual devotion with manual labor, thereby sanctifying the act of creation itself.

Benedictine monasteries emerged as centers of learning and artistic production during the Middle Ages, a period often mischaracterized as the 'Dark Ages.' Contrary to this misnomer, these monasteries were beacons of light that preserved and advanced human knowledge. They became the custodians of cultural heritage, meticulously copying ancient manuscripts that might have otherwise been lost to the ravages of time and tumult (Leclercq, 1989).

The scriptoria of these monasteries were not merely places of transcription but vibrant studios of innovation, where monks would illuminate manuscripts with intricate designs and vivid colors. These illuminated manuscripts, such as the famous Book of Kells, are testament to the Benedictines' reverence for the Word of God, which they adorned with the utmost care and creativity (Backhouse, 1981).

But the Benedictine contribution extends beyond the preservation and embellishment of texts. Their architectural endeavors, seen in the majestic simplicity of their abbeys, articulate a theology of space where form follows faith. The construction of the Abbey of Cluny, for instance, represents an apex of Romanesque architecture, harmonizing physical grandeur with spiritual aspiration (Conant, 1973).

In the realm of music, the Benedictines played a pivotal role in the development of Gregorian chant, an art form that epitomizes the sacred synthesis of beauty and truth. This chant, characterized by its meditative and pure melodies, facilitated communal prayer and liturgical ceremony, binding individual souls to the divine (Hiley, 1993).

This ethos of integration between work and worship further propelled the Benedictines into the realm of agriculture, craftsmanship, and brewing. By treating these activities as forms of prayer, the Benedictines harnessed creativity to foster communities that were self-sufficient, thus weaving a holistic tapestry of spiritual and material sustenance.

Moreover, the Benedictine commitment to hospitality has also left a rich cultural legacy. Their monasteries have served as places of rest, reflection, and rejuvenation for travelers, scholars, and pilgrims, thereby facilitating a cross-pollination of ideas and artistic influences that have enriched the Catholic intellectual and aesthetic tradition.

The education provided by Benedictine monasteries played a crucial role in the intellectual revival of Europe. Their schools were among the first to provide a systematic curriculum outside the familial context, emphasizing the liberal arts as a foundation for both spiritual and intellectual growth (Leclercq, 1989).

In essence, the Benedictines mastered the art of living within the temporal world while not being of it. By consecrating every aspect of daily life to God, they exemplified how the act of creation is both a reflection and a participation in the divine creative act. This perspective sanctified the mundane, thereby revealing the sacramental nature of the world.

The Benedictines also contributed significantly to the preservation of nature and the promotion of agriculture as a reflection of God's bounty. Their monastic gardens, which provided both sustenance and a space for contemplation, symbolize the harmonious relationship between human beings and creation.

The Order's commitment to education and the transmission of culture was further mirrored in their role as pioneers of the university system. The establishment of these centers of higher learning under Benedictine guidance was instrumental in the shaping of Western intellectual tradition.

Through the ages, Benedictine artistry has never been an end in itself but a means of transcending the temporal to touch the eternal. Every brush stroke, every note of chant, and every stone laid was imbued with a deep sense of purpose—to glorify God and lead the human spirit towards Him.

Today, the legacy of the Benedictines continues to inspire both religious and secular communities. In an age often characterized by fragmentation and superficiality, the Benedictine model of integrating prayer, work, and community life offers a blueprint for cultural renewal anchored in transcendent values.

In conclusion, the Benedictine contribution to art and culture is a testament to the transformative power of integrating faith with all aspects of human creativity and work. Their legacy, characterized by a profound union of the sacred and the profane, continues to illuminate the path towards a more holistic and sacred vision of creation.

Through their enduring commitment to the sanctification of the ordinary, the Benedictines have eloquently articulated a vision of art and culture that transcends time. In their monasteries, scriptoria, and schools, they have crafted a legacy that endures as a beacon of beauty, wisdom, and holiness in the ever-changing landscape of human history.

Franciscans, Dominicans, and Jesuits: Varied Visions of Beauty

As we delve into the heart of the Catholic tradition's artistic legacy, it becomes paramount to explore the distinctive contributions of three influential religious orders: the Franciscans, Dominicans, and Jesuits. Each of these communities has fostered a unique approach to beauty, deeply rooted in their spiritual ethos and theological foundations, crafting a rich tapestry of the Catholic aesthetic imagination.

The Franciscans, founded by St. Francis of Assisi in the early 13th century, have championed a vision of beauty that is profoundly incarnational and creation-centered. St. Francis, known for his deep love of creation and commitment to poverty, saw the reflection of God's beauty in all aspects of the natural world and in the faces of the poor and marginalized. Franciscan art, therefore, embodies simplicity, humility, and a profound sense of joy in God's creation. The portrayal of St. Francis in art, from the frescoes of Giotto in the Basilica of St. Francis of Assisi to contemporary depictions, emphasizes this joy and humility, inviting onlookers into a deeper appreciation of God's presence in the world around us.

Distinctly different, the Dominicans, founded by St. Dominic in the early 13th century, cultivated an intellectual and preaching-oriented spirituality. This charism profoundly influenced their approach to beauty. The Dominican artistic tradition is marked by a deep commitment to the proclamation of truth through beauty.

Illuminated manuscripts, such as the Saint Dominic's own Nine Ways of Prayer, and the works of Fra Angelico, a Dominican friar, exemplify this vision. Fra Angelico's frescoes in the convent of San Marco in Florence are famed for their theological depth, capturing complex dogmatic truths with sublime beauty, thus serving as a form of visual preaching.

Enter the Jesuits, or the Society of Jesus, founded in the 16th century by St. Ignatius of Loyola. The Jesuits introduced a dynamic and adaptive approach to beauty, reflecting their broader mission to "find God in all things." Jesuit art and architecture, evident in the works within the Church of the Gesù in Rome or the richly decorated missions in South America, are characterized by grandeur, emotional depth, and a sense of upward movement, directing the viewer's gaze towards the divine. The Jesuit commitment to education and the global dimension of their mission also led to a significant cross-cultural artistic exchange, enriching the Catholic artistic tradition with diverse expressions of beauty.

The varied visions of beauty espoused by the Franciscans, Dominicans, and Jesuits, reflect a deeper theological and spiritual truth: that beauty is a pathway to encountering God. In Franciscan simplicity and reverence for creation, in Dominican illumination of truth through beauty, and in Jesuit grandeur and universality, we see different facets of God's infinite beauty. These artistic expressions not only enrich the Church's liturgical life and devotional practices but also serve as powerful mediums of evangelization and catechesis.

Moreover, the contributions of these orders underscore the incarnational aspect of Catholic art. Just as the Word became flesh and dwelt among us, so too does Catholic art make the divine tangible, accessible, and relatable. Whether through a simple fresco that captures the humility of St. Francis, a theologically rich painting that articulates Dominican preaching, or a grand Jesuit church that lifts the soul to God, each artistic expression invites the faithful into a deeper relationship with the divine.

The Franciscans remind us that beauty is found in poverty, humility, and the natural world; the Dominicans, that beauty and truth are inseparable; and the Jesuits, that beauty is dynamic, universal, and capable of transcending cultural boundaries. These varied visions not only contribute to the richness of the Catholic artistic tradition but also offer distinct pathways for the faithful to encounter and engage with the divine.

In our contemporary world, where beauty is often commodified or reduced to mere aesthetics, the Franciscan, Dominican, and Jesuit visions of beauty challenge us to see beauty as a reflection of God's glory and love. They call us to a deeper appreciation of the sacred in the ordinary, the power of beauty to convey truth, and the universal call to find God in all things.

As we continue to explore the symphony of Catholic art, it becomes evident that the Franciscan, Dominican, and Jesuit contributions underscore the Church's mission to evangelize through beauty. In a world hungry for meaning and transcendence, the artistic legacy of these orders offers a beacon of hope, pointing towards the ultimate source of beauty: God Himself.

In conclusion, the Franciscans, Dominicans, and Jesuits, through their distinct spiritualities, have enriched the Catholic artistic tradition with varied visions of beauty. These visions not only highlight the transcendental beauty of God but also serve as a testament to the enduring power of art as a medium for divine encounter and spiritual transformation. In their differences, these orders embody the universality of the Church and its mission to bring the beauty of the Gospel to every corner of the world.

Chapter 15: Iconography: Windows to Heaven

Across the span of centuries, the tradition of iconography within the Catholic Church has stood as a testament to the profound capacity of art to bridge the finite and the infinite, the human and the divine. In this exploration of iconography as "Windows to Heaven," we delve into an art form that embodies the very essence of Catholic imagination and theological vision. The realm of iconography is not merely an artistic expression but an invitation into the mystical participation in the sacred mysteries it represents.

The genesis of iconography can be traced back to the early Christian centuries, emerging prominently within the Eastern traditions of the Church. Here, icons were not seen as mere decorations or artistic endeavors but as theological statements in and of themselves, conveying truths about God, the saints, and the mysteries of faith with a language that transcends words (Ouspensky & Lossky, 1982). The theology of icons is deeply rooted in the Incarnation, the belief that in becoming man, God made it possible for the material world to convey spiritual realities.

At the heart of iconography lies a profound affirmation of the material world as a vessel for divine grace. Icons serve as tangible points of contact between the believer and the holy figures they depict, integrating the spiritual and material realms in a harmonious union. This integration reflects the broader Catholic understanding of sacramentality, where physical elements are endowed with a spiritual significance that leads the soul closer to the divine mystery.

The veneration of icons, sometimes misunderstood, is not an act of idolatry but of honor directed towards the person depicted. It's a recognition of the icon as a sacred window through which the faithful may enter into a deeper communion with the saints and the Divine. By venerating icons, believers participate in the reality to which the icon points, drawing near to the heavenly kingdom here and now.

The creation of an icon is itself a spiritual exercise, undertaken with prayer and fasting. The iconographer engages in a process that is as much about cultivating personal holiness as it is about artistic skill. This process underscores the idea that beauty and artistic talent are gifts from God, meant to draw both creator and beholder closer to the divine (Sendler, 1988). It is this intrinsic connection between spirituality and artistry that characterizes iconography as a unique form of divine labor.

The distinct style of icons, with their deliberate use of color, perspective, and symbolism, serves a specific theological purpose. The stylized features and lack of naturalistic perspective are not due to an absence of skill, but a conscious effort to transcend the temporal and reach for the eternal. As such, icons present the holy figures not as they were in their earthly existence but as they are in the glorified state, emphasizing their sanctity and their participation in the divine life.

The use of light and color in iconography carries deep theological significance. Gold, often used to depict the background, signifies the uncreated light of God, illuminating the saint or the scene from beyond the visible world. The colors are not chosen at random but are loaded with symbolic meaning, conveying theological truths about the nature of the divine and the spiritual journey of the soul.

One cannot discuss the significance of iconography without mentioning the pivotal role of the iconostasis in Eastern liturgical tradition. This wall of icons, separating the nave from the sanctuary in Orthodox and Eastern Catholic churches, serves not as a barrier but as a point of connection between the congregation and the mysteries taking place at the altar. The iconostasis embodies the theology of iconography, making visible the heavenly hosts that join the faithful in worship.

The tradition of iconography extends beyond the East, influencing Western Catholic art as well. While the stylistic expressions may differ, the underlying theological principles find resonance across both traditions, reflecting a shared belief in the transformative power of beauty and art to convey divine truths.

The icon's role in personal devotion and liturgical life continues to be a vital aspect of Catholic spirituality. Icons are not merely objects of art; they are conduits of grace, instruments through which individuals and communities encounter the sacred. They remind us that heaven is not a distant reality but one intimately connected to the material world, accessible through the windows of iconography.

In the modern era, the significance of iconography endures, perhaps even grows, as believers and seekers alike navigate a world often divorced from the sense of the sacred. Icons stand as beacons of the divine, inviting all to gaze upon the holy and find solace, inspiration, and a call to deeper faith.

The journey through the "Windows to Heaven" that iconography provides is not merely an aesthetic experience but a theological voyage. It invites a contemplative gaze, not just with the eyes but with the heart, encouraging a silent encounter with the divine that speaks directly to the soul. In this silent contemplation, the viewer is drawn into the mystery depicted, transcending time and space, to touch the eternal.

The tradition of iconography, with its profound theological and spiritual dimensions, serves as a foundational pillar in the edifice of Catholic art. It exemplifies the Catholic imagination's ability to see beyond the visible, to find in the created world a reflection of the divine. Iconography challenges and inspires, calling believers to a deeper appreciation of the mystery of faith, made visible through the artistry of sanctified imagination.

In conclusion, iconography remains one of the most powerful expressions of Catholic theology and spirituality, a true "Window to Heaven." Through this sacred art, the faithful are invited to glimpse the divine reality that lies beyond the sensory world. As we continue to explore the vast domain of Catholic art, may the tradition of iconography serve as a constant reminder of the capacity of beauty to elevate the human spirit to the divine.

The Tradition of Icons in the Catholic East

In the luminous expanse of the Catholic East, icons stand as profound expressions of faith and theology, encapsulated in visual form. These sacred images, venerated across generations, serve not merely as religious decorations but as windows to the divine, embodying the spiritual realm in a way that is accessible and profound. The tradition of iconography, deeply embedded in Eastern Catholic and Orthodox Christian traditions, offers a unique insight into the divine mystery, inviting the faithful into a direct, contemplative relationship with the holy.

At the heart of Eastern iconography lies the conviction that icons are more than art; they are a sacramental presence, where Heaven touches earth. This belief is founded upon the Incarnation of Christ, the Word made flesh, which sanctifies material creation as a vessel of divine grace. Just as Christ is the Image (Icon) of the invisible God, so too icons function as tangible manifestations of the spiritual world, offering glimpses into the heavenly kingdom and facilitating personal encounters with the saints and the Divine.

The creation of an icon is itself considered a form of prayer, a liturgical act that echoes the work of creation. Iconographers approach their work with fasting, prayer, and a deep sense of humility, understanding their role as mediators of divine truths. These artists, often anonymous, relinquish personal acclaim, focusing instead on their service to God and the Church. The guidelines for creating an icon are rigorous, adhering to canonical forms that have been passed down through centuries, ensuring theological accuracy and spiritual depth.

Icons are consecrated objects, blessed and venerated in liturgical contexts, emphasizing their spiritual utility over their aesthetic value. The veneration of icons, misunderstood by some as idolatry, is firmly rooted in the distinction between worship due to God alone and the veneration offered to saints and holy images. This practice is encapsulated in the Seventh Ecumenical Council (Nicaea II, 787), which defended the veneration of icons as an affirmation of the Incarnation and a rejection of iconoclasm, thereby cementing the role of icons in Orthodox Christian and Eastern Catholic spirituality.

The most sacred icons often depict Christ, the Theotokos (Mother of God), and the saints, each character being portrayed with symbolic attributes that convey their spiritual significance. The style of these icons, characterized by a profound stillness and a sense of otherworldly beauty, eschews naturalism for a spiritual symbolism that enlightens the mind and elevates the soul. The use of inverse perspective, where lines converge not on the horizon but on the viewer, invites participation in the depicted mystery, making the viewer a part of the icon's sacred narrative.

Throughout history, certain icons have been attributed with miraculous powers, becoming centers of pilgrimage and devotion. These wonderworking icons, through their association with healings and divine interventions, remind the faithful of the active presence of God and His saints in the world. Such icons, venerated across the Catholic East, stand as testament to the enduring power of sacred art to inspire faith, offer solace, and facilitate encounters with the divine.

In modern times, the tradition of iconography has experienced a resurgence, both in the East and increasingly in the Western Church, as a testament to the universality and timeless relevance of icons. This revival speaks to a growing recognition of beauty and sacred art's capacity to transcend cultural and denominational boundaries, uniting believers in the shared experience of divine mystery.

The influence of Eastern iconography extends beyond the confines of liturgy and devotion, impacting religious art worldwide. The theology and aesthetics of icons have inspired countless artists, fostering a dialogue between tradition and innovation. In the process, these sacred images continue to reveal the depth of God's love, manifesting the divine in forms that speak to the heart of the faithful across ages and cultures.

As windows to Heaven, icons remain a vital part of the Church's life, teaching, and tradition—a heritage of faith that is both ancient and ever new. They are constant reminders of the Church's sacramental vision, where the material world is transfigured by grace, and the human encounter with the divine is mediated through beauty. In this sense, icons are not merely artifacts of religious tradition but vibrant expressions of the Church's ongoing pilgrimage toward the Kingdom of God, where the Image (Icon) of the invisible is fully revealed.

The Theology of Icons Within the resplendent tapestry of Catholic art, icons stand as a solemn testament to the divine mystery that permeates human history. These sacred images, more than mere artwork, are theological statements, steeped in the rich tradition of the Church's Eastern rites. They serve not only as objects of veneration but also as vibrant portals to the divine, inviting the faithful into a deeper communion with God. The theology of icons, hence, becomes a crucial element in understanding the interplay between divine revelation and human creativity, encapsulated in these holy images.

In the theology of icons, the concept of 'veneration' is distinct from 'worship.' Veneration (proskynesis) is accorded to icons, while worship (latreia) is reserved for the Triune God alone. This distinction is pivotal, underscoring the role of icons not as idols but as windows to heaven, facilitating a rendezvous with the divine. The Seventh Ecumenical Council (Nicaea II, 787), which affirmed the veneration of icons, articulated that through icons, the faithful are lifted to the contemplation of the realities they portray (Mondzain, 2005).

Icons, in their essence, are didactic; they teach the faithful about the mysteries of the faith. This educational role is rooted in the Incarnation itself. Just as the Word became flesh and dwelt among us (John 1:14), making the invisible God visible, icons make tangible the spiritual realities they represent. They are, therefore, not mere decorations but catechetical tools, leading the faithful to a deeper understanding of the faith.

The creation of an icon is considered a liturgical act, a sacred process that involves prayer and fasting. The iconographer, working in the tradition of the early Church Fathers, is seen as a vessel through which divine grace flows, translating sacred truths into visual form. This calls for a profound spirituality and adherence to the canons and traditions that have guided iconography for centuries. The preparation of materials, the application of colors, and even the act of painting are imbued with prayer, rendering the creation of an icon a form of worship.

Central to the theology of icons is the concept of 'presence.' Icons are not considered to be simple representations but rather manifestations of the person depicted. They remind the faithful that Christ and the saints are truly present with them. This presence is not symbolic but real, albeit in a different mode of existence. Thus, when one venerates an icon, one is venerating the person it depicts, entering into a communion with them.

The colors and symbols used in icons carry profound theological meanings. Gold, often used as a background, symbolizes the divine glory and heaven. Blue represents the humanity of Christ and the Theotokos, while red signifies divine life. The stylized features and absence of perspective aim not to depict earthly reality but a transformed, heavenly reality, free from the corruption of sin. This eschews naturalism in favor of a spiritual aesthetic that transcends time and space, drawing the viewer into the eternal.

The role of light in icons is particularly noteworthy. Unlike in Western art, where light typically emanates from a single, external source, light in icons appears to emanate from within the subjects themselves. This reflects the theological truth that Christ is the Light of the World, illuminating all of creation. It signifies the uncreated light of God, visible to the purified heart, as experienced by the saints during the Transfiguration of Christ.

Icons of the Theotokos, or the Mother of God, hold a special place in the theology of icons. Often depicted pointing to her Son, she is presented not only as the Mother of God but as the Hodegetria, she who shows the way. This iconography underscores the pivotal role of the Theotokos in the salvation narrative, leading the faithful to Christ.

The veneration of icons has also been a source of controversy, notably during the Iconoclast Controversy in the 8th and 9th centuries. The defenders of icons, known as Iconodules, argued that the condemnation of icons amounted to a denial of the Incarnation, the central mystery of the Christian faith. They maintained that if God could assume flesh and be depicted, then the veneration of these depictions was not only permissible but necessary, affirming the truth of God's closeness to humanity.

The reconciliation of the Church with the veneration of icons was not merely an affirmation of art but a profound theological statement about the nature of Christ and His relationship with creation. It illuminated the Incarnation's cosmic significance, affirming that matter could be sanctified and become a vehicle of divine grace. Icons, in this light, are seen as a reaffirmation of the goodness of creation and a testament to the redemptive work of Christ.

The 'reverse perspective' employed in many icons, where lines converge not on the horizon but on the viewer, serves to involve the viewer in the depicted scene. It breaks down the barrier between the sacred and the profane, inviting the viewer to step into the divine reality portrayed in the icon. This theological and artistic technique illustrates the Church's understanding of salvation as a participatory process, engaging the whole person in a journey toward the divine.

Moreover, icons are integral to the liturgical life of the Church. During the Divine Liturgy, icons surround the faithful, not as mere observers but as participants in the heavenly worship. This 'cloud of witnesses' reminds the faithful of their connection to the Communion of Saints, transcending geographical and temporal boundaries. The iconostasis, a wall of icons separating the nave from the sanctuary, serves as a symbolic threshold between heaven and earth, bridging the chasm sin has wrought.

In conclusion, the theology of icons reveals the profound depth and beauty of the Christian vision of reality. Through their creation and veneration, icons teach, sanctify, and lead the faithful into the mystery of the Incarnation and the communion of saints. They stand as vibrant testimonies to the truth that all creation is called to reflect the glory of God, drawing all who gaze upon them into a deeper encounter with the living God.

Chapter 16: The Light of Faith: Stained Glass and Sacred Art

In the mosaic of Catholic tradition, stained glass windows illuminate the sacred narratives with a vibrancy that transcends mere illustration. These radiant panels are not solely decorative but serve as catechismal tools, embodying the theological virtues of faith, hope, and charity. Through the alchemy of light and color, stained glass transforms the sun's rays into narratives that edify the viewer, integrating scriptural stories with the experience of divine transcendence.

The craft of stained glass, refined through centuries, involves a union of artistic skill and spiritual contemplation. Artisans of this medium become theologians with glass and lead, their work a silent yet eloquent sermon. Techniques passed down through generations—such as the selection of pigmented glass, firing methods to achieve precise hues, and leading compositions—remain testimony to a lineage of devotion. These craftsmen and women encode symbolism within each piece, turning each window into a lexicon of Christian iconography.

Yet, the significance of stained glass extends beyond the walls of cathedrals and churches. This art form represents a crucial intersection of human creativity and divine inspiration. It stands as a monument to the Catholic imagination, which envisions the world illuminated by the light of faith. Each window offers a vision of creation suffused with the glory of God, inviting contemplation and prayer. The vibrant hues and intricate designs encapsulate moments of salvation history, rendering the invisible God visible to the human eye. As sunlight shifts, so do the stories told by each pane, reminding us of the ever-changing yet constant presence of God in our lives.

Contemplating stained glass windows, the faithful are drawn into a meditative journey. This journey mirrors the path of salvation— where light breaks through darkness, and chaos gives way to harmony. In the silent contemplation of these sacred artworks, one finds a microcosm of the Church's pilgrimage toward the eternal light. Here, art converges with faith, and beauty serves as a conduit for divine grace. It echoes the call to conversion, where each beam of light invites the soul to turn towards the source of all beauty and truth.

The legacy of stained glass, thus, transcends mere artistry; it embodies the Church's mission to evangelize through beauty. As the faithful gaze upon these illuminated stories, they are not only reminded of the past deeds of saints and saviors but are also inspired to carry forward the light of Christ in their own lives. In the resplendence of stained glass, we find a visual hymn of praise to the Creator, a testimony to the enduring power of faith rendered in color and light.

The Storytelling Power of Stained Glass

Within the sacred halls of cathedrals and churches, stained glass windows do not merely serve as decor but as profound narratives of faith, capturing the essence of biblical stories and the virtues of saints through vibrant colors and light. This form of sacred art transcends mere visual appreciation, engaging the faithful in a silent dialogue that bridges the chasm between the divine and the human, illuminating minds and enkindling hearts with the light of faith.

The technique of creating stained glass, a masterful embrace of artistry and technical skill, has been refined over centuries, becoming a distinctive feature of Gothic and later architectural styles. The artisans of stained glass serve as silent theologians, translating divine mysteries into a language of color and light, accessible to all who gaze upon their work. This symbiosis of art and faith embodies the Church's dedication to the evangelization and catechesis of the populace, adhering to the principle that beauty serves as a pathway to understanding and embracing the divine.

Stained glass windows often encapsulate biblical narratives or representations of saints, offering visual sermons that elucidate the virtues of faith, hope, and charity. They act as catechetical tools, edifying the faithful and introducing the uninitiated to the depth of Christian doctrine and history. Through these luminous portals, stories unfold in a spectrum of colors, each hue holding symbolic significance, guiding the contemplative soul on a journey of spiritual discovery and enlightenment.

In the medieval period, when literacy was not widespread, stained glass windows played a crucial role in the education of the laity about the scriptures and the lives of the saints. This tradition persists, reinforcing the timeless relevance of these stories and the enduring need for visual representations of the faith in an increasingly post-literate digital age. The light filtering through the stained glass embodies the divine light of God, breaking into the darkness of the world, inviting those within the sacred space to lift their minds and hearts to things above.

Consider the intricate stained glass windows of Chartres Cathedral or the Sainte-Chapelle in Paris, where the celestial light transforms the interior ambiance, captivating the viewer's senses and elevating the spirit. The narrative complexity within these windows serves not only as an artistic achievement but as a testament to the intricate tapestry of faith woven into the fabric of the Catholic Church. Each window tells a story, each figure a sermon in light, guiding the faithful through the mysteries of the Christian faith.

The storytelling power of stained glass is an invitation to enter into a meditative state, contemplating the divine mysteries that these vibrant windows seek to unveil. They are a call to prayer, a reminder of the presence of God, and a manifestation of the Holy Spirit moving through light and color. The experience of beholding these windows can move the soul to awe, inspiring a profound encounter with the sacred that transcends the limitations of language.

Stained glass windows embody the Church's understanding that beauty is a vital instrument of God's revelation. Through their storytelling power, they evangelize, teach, and inspire, serving as luminous signposts on the path to salvation. Indeed, they are a form of sacred scripture written in light, a testament to the enduring truth that in beauty, one can find a reflection of the divine.

In contemporary times, the art of stained glass continues to evolve, with artists exploring new techniques and themes that speak to the modern faithful while continuing the tradition of storytelling that has characterized this art form for centuries. Despite changes in style and method, the essence of stained glass as a conduit of divine light and truth remains undiminished, testifying to the timeless relevance of sacred art in the life of the Church.

The stained glass window, then, stands as a potent symbol of faith's light shining through the complexities of human history, illuminating our path with stories of salvation, grace, and redemption. In their silent beauty, these windows call to us across the ages, inviting us to reflect on our place within the divine narrative and encouraging us to continue our journey towards the eternal light.

In conclusion, the storytelling power of stained glass in sacred spaces not only enriches the aesthetic landscape of the Church but also deepens the spiritual life of the faithful. As windows to heaven, stained glass artistry continues to shine as a beacon of faith, hope, and love, guiding generations toward divine truth. In their resplendent light, we are reminded of the Church's mission to bring Christ to the world and to unveil the splendor of His love through the medium of beauty.

Techniques and Symbolism In the realm of stained glass and sacred art, the confluence of artistic skill, theological insight, and symbolic depth crafts a narrative that transcends the visible, touching upon the divine. This section delves into the nuanced interplay between techniques and symbolism in stained glass artistry, as applied within the Catholic tradition, illuminating its profound role in spiritual storytelling and liturgical life.

The genesis of stained glass as an art form is rooted in a synthesis of technological innovation and spiritual aspiration. The method of adding metallic oxides to glass during its manufacture produces vibrant colors that, when assembled into complex designs, articulate stories, doctrines, and heavenly visions. The very essence of light, transformed through these colored panes, becomes a metaphor for divine presence—transcendent, yet intimately intersecting with human experience.

Symbolism in stained glass art is both universal and particular; certain themes and motifs recur across time and space, while others are deeply contextual, reflecting the specificities of local cultures, hagiographies, and theological emphases. Central to Catholic iconography are the representations of Christ, the Virgin Mary, the saints, and the narratives of salvation history. Each figure, each scene is imbued with layers of meaning, inviting contemplation and devotion.

The portrayal of Christ, for instance, encompasses a spectrum from the Good Shepherd to the suffering Servant, from the King of Kings to the Lamb of God. These images not only depict various aspects of Christ's identity and mission but also invite the faithful into a relationship with Him, mediated by light and color. The figure of Mary, too, is depicted in myriad forms—Mater Dolorosa, Queen of Heaven, Immaculate Conception—each articulating elements of doctrine and devotion through visual means.

Beyond these central figures, the stories told through stained glass windows often include scenes from the Bible, moments of sacramental significance, and events from the lives of saints. Here, the technique of leading—the use of lead strips to join pieces of colored glass—plays a vital role in delineating details, shaping narratives, and creating a visual coherence that guides the viewer's gaze across the unfolding tableau.

The interaction of light with stained glass introduces a dynamic element to these narratives. Depending upon the time of day, season, or weather, the intensity and quality of light passing through the windows vary, suggesting the ever-changing presence of the Divine in the midst of creation. This ephemeral quality emphasizes the notion of sacred time, the liturgical calendar becoming visually represented in the waxing and waning luminosity of these artworks.

Architectural considerations also inform the placement and themes of stained glass windows. The orientation of a church, the function of specific spaces within it, and the architectural style all play roles in determining how and where windows are situated, and what they depict. Thus, the art of stained glass is inextricably linked to the sacred architecture that houses it, both shaping and being shaped by its spatial context.

Over the centuries, the techniques involved in creating stained glass have evolved, from the medieval pot metal glass to the enamel painting of the Renaissance, and onwards to the innovative methods of the modern era. Despite these technological shifts, the core intention—using light, color, and form to convey spiritual truths—remains constant. Contemporary artists working in stained glass continue to explore this rich vein of sacred art, drawing on traditional themes while also engaging with the concerns of the modern world.

One of the challenges faced by artists and patrons of stained glass is the preservation of ancient windows, many of which have suffered from environmental exposure, vandalism, or simply the ravages of time. Restoration efforts require a delicate balance between technical proficiency and sensitivity to historical and spiritual significance, aiming to retain the original intent and beauty of these works while ensuring their continued presence.

In a broader cultural context, stained glass windows stand as witnesses to the enduring human quest for transcendence. They are visible sermons, narrative tapestries woven from light and glass, inviting not just the faithful but all who behold them to ponder the mysteries they embody. In this sense, the art of stained glass serves not only a liturgical function but also an evangelistic one, drawing viewers into the story of faith that lies at the heart of Catholicism.

The symbiosis of technique and symbolism in stained glass is a testament to the Catholic imagination, which sees in the material world a window to the divine. It reflects a sacramental worldview, where ordinary elements—glass, lead, light—are transformed into means of grace, mediating the presence of God to His people. In this way, stained glass art serves as a microcosm of Catholic artistic endeavor, marrying beauty with truth, and creation with Creator.

In conclusion, the study of techniques and symbolism in stained glass offers profound insights into the Catholic artistic tradition. It reveals the depth of thought, the richness of faith, and the heights of creativity that characterize this enduring form of sacred art. In each pane, in each ray of light refracted, lies an invitation to gaze deeper—not only at the art itself but through it, to the eternal Light it seeks to manifest.

Chapter 17: Vestments and Sacred Vessels: The Fabric of Worship

The communion of the faithful with the divine finds its most profound expression within the liturgy, a realm where the aesthetic elements serve not merely as decorations but as silent teachers of the eternal. Vestments and sacred vessels, in their sheer beauty and solemnity, transcend their physical nature to become part of the living tradition of the Church, embodying the sacred mysteries they serve. This chapter explores the vital role that these elements play in the fabric of worship, weaving a narrative that connects the material to the spiritual, the human to the divine.

In the panoply of Catholic worship, vestments function as more than ceremonial attire. They are imbued with symbolism and significance, echoing the sacramental grace they seek to manifest. Each piece, from the stole representing the yoke of Christ to the chasuble symbolizing charity, tells a part of the salvific story. These garments, in their colors and styles, follow the rhythm of the liturgical calendar, marking the seasons of celebration, penance, and reflection within the Church's year.

Sacred vessels, contrived from materials that range from humble clay to precious metals, hold within them not just the elements of Eucharist but also the prayers and aspirations of the faithful. The chalice and paten, objects of both beauty and purpose, are consecrated for the solemn act of the Eucharist, making present the

Last Supper and the Sacrifice on the Cross. The meticulous care in their creation and maintenance speaks to the reverence accorded to the Real Presence they hold.

The beauty of liturgical arts, manifest in vestments and sacred vessels, serves as a testament to the Church's understanding of beauty as a path to God. In a world often marred by the ephemeral and the mundane, these elements stand as beacons of the eternal, drawing believers into a deeper communion with the divine. They are not mere adornments but participants in the sacred mysteries, enhancing the liturgical experience and elevating hearts and minds to contemplation.

Symbolism runs deep in the design and use of liturgical objects. Each fabric pattern on a vestment, each inscription on a chalice, is laden with theological meaning, offering silent catechesis to those who partake in the liturgy. The juxtaposition of the human craftsmanship and divine service, encapsulated in these objects, reflects the Church's sacramental vision where the material world is suffused with spiritual significance.

The evolution of liturgical vestments and vessels across centuries showcases the Church's ability to honor tradition while engaging with the changing contexts of history and culture. This adaptability ensures that the sacred mysteries they serve remain accessible and meaningful to every generation, signifying the universality and timelessness of the Catholic faith.

Empowered by the Church's teachings, artists and craftsmen who create these sacred items participate in a form of ministry, contributing their talents to the glorification of God and the sanctification of the faithful. Their work is a form of prayer, a physical manifestation of their devotion and their cooperation with divine grace.

Moreover, the liturgical use of vestments and vessels sanctifies human labor, elevating the work of hands to an offering pleasing to God. This sanctification of labor resonates with the Church's social teaching, emphasizing the dignity of work and the worker in the divine plan.

In contemporary times, the challenge emerges to preserve the beauty and significance of these liturgical elements amid trends that favor minimalism or secular aesthetics. The Church remains a guardian of sacred beauty, ensuring that the liturgical arts continue to reflect the splendor of the divine and the depth of the mysteries celebrated.

As the faithful gather around the altar, vestments and sacred vessels serve as visual sermons, silent yet eloquent testimonials of faith. They are part of the Church's living tradition, ever ancient and ever new, inviting believers to experience the sacred through the sensory, drawing them closer to the mystery of the divine made present in the liturgy.

This chapter, in examining the role of vestments and sacred vessels in worship, invites a deeper appreciation for these elements as expressions of the Church's faith and artistry. In understanding their significance, believers are reminded of the beauty of worship, the profundity of the sacraments, and the grace that flows when the fabric of creation is woven with the divine.

This exploration would be incomplete without acknowledging the sources that have enriched our understanding of liturgical arts. Duffy et al. (1991) provide a comprehensive overview of the historical development and theological significance of sacred vestments in their work, underscoring the depth of symbolism woven into the fabric of worship. Lang (2004) offers a detailed examination of the evolution of liturgical vessels, highlighting their artistic and religious importance in the Catholic tradition. Lastly, the contribution of cannot be overlooked, as her study on the emotions conveyed through liturgical objects opens up new avenues for understanding the experiential aspect of worship. Through these works, the richness of the Church's liturgical heritage is brought to light, offering a foundation upon which to build a deeper appreciation for the fabric of worship.

The Beauty of Liturgical Arts

In the heart of worship within the Catholic tradition lies a rich tapestry symbolized through liturgical arts, a silent yet eloquent testimony to the profundity of the faith's sacramental vision. The vestments worn by priests and deacons, along with the sacred vessels utilized during the Eucharistic celebration, are not mere accessories but are imbued with deep theological and spiritual meanings. These elements of the liturgy are not only functional but serve as visual catechisms, teaching and drawing the faithful into a deeper understanding and appreciation of the mysteries being celebrated.

The origins of liturgical vestments trace back to the garments of the ancient world, evolving over centuries to embody the dignity and solemnity of the liturgical rites. Each element, from the alb to the chasuble, and from the stole to the cincture, carries with it a symbolism that echoes the scriptural foundations of the priestly ministry. These garments, often richly adorned and carefully crafted, stand as a testament to the beauty and holiness of the actions being performed, transforming the celebrant from an individual to an icon of Christ himself, the High Priest.

Similarly, the sacred vessels - the chalice, paten, ciborium, and more - are crafted with the utmost care, typically from precious metals, to honor the Real Presence of Christ in the Eucharist. The design and artistry of these vessels serve to elevate the mind and heart to the sacred, reminding all of the treasure they contain: the very Body and Blood, Soul and Divinity of Jesus Christ. The use of beautiful and precious materials underscores the value of what is celebrated and received in the sacred liturgy.

This elevation of the mundane to the realm of the sacred is a core aspect of Catholic theology - the sacramentality that sees the whole created world as capable of bearing the divine. The liturgical arts, in their beauty and complexity, are a microcosm of this vision, where even the simplest of elements are transformed into vehicles of grace. Here lies a profound catechesis on the Incarnation itself, as material elements - bread, wine, fabric, and metal - become bearers of the Divine.

The designing and crafting of liturgical items is itself a form of worship, a vocation that demands not only artistic skill but also a deep spirituality. Artists and artisans who work in this realm participate in a sacred trust, serving the liturgy by providing elements that speak not only to the minds of the faithful but also to their hearts, drawing them into a deeper communion with God. Their work is a blend of prayer and labor, each stitch and hammer blow an act of devotion to the God of beauty and truth.

Moreover, the diversity found in liturgical arts across cultures and history speaks to the catholicity - the universality - of the Church. While there exists a harmonious unity in the fundamental aspects of liturgical attire and vessels, there is also a beautiful variety that reflects the myriad ways in which different cultures express their reverence towards the sacred. This diversity is not a source of division but a testament to the Church's ability to inculturate the Gospel message in every time and place, making the unchanging truths of faith resonate in every heart.

In the liturgical arts, the Church finds a powerful means of evangelization. For many, the beauty encountered in a well-arranged liturgy or the craftsmanship of sacred vessels can be a pathway to encountering God. The transcendental beauty, which points beyond itself to the Divine, can awaken in the human heart a recognition of the presence of God and stir a desire for communion with Him. In this way, the liturgical arts serve not only those already within the Church but also reach out to those who are searching, offering them a glimpse of the heavenly reality.

The care and expense invested in these sacred objects also reflect the value the Church places on the liturgy as the "source and summit" of Christian life (Vatican II, Lumen Gentium). In a culture that often values utility over beauty, the Church's commitment to the aesthetic quality of liturgical elements is a powerful counter-sign, affirming the intrinsic worth of beauty and its capacity to convey spiritual truths.

The formation of those who craft these sacred objects is therefore of paramount importance. It is essential that artisans understand not only the technical aspects of their craft but also the liturgical and theological principles that inform their work. A deep liturgical formation ensures that their creations are not only aesthetically pleasing but also truly serve the liturgy in enhancing the prayerful participation of the faithful.

The stewardship of liturgical arts also involves careful preservation and maintenance. Many vestments and vessels are historic, handed down through generations and carrying with them the stories of faith communities across the ages. Their preservation is a testament to the continuity of the faith, a tangible link to the Church triumphant that spans across time and space. In this sense, they are not only functional items but also sacred heirlooms that carry the spiritual heritage of the Church.

In conclusion, the beauty of liturgical arts serves a dual purpose: it glorifies God and sanctifies the faithful. Through these sacred objects, the Church communicates the mystery of the sacred liturgy, making visible the invisible realities of our faith. They are an integral part of the fabric of worship, woven from threads of tradition, beauty, and devotion. As such, they call us to a deeper awareness of the sacred, inviting us to enter more fully into the mystery of our redemption through the liturgical rites.

Symbolism in Liturgical Objects In the celebration of the liturgy, every detail holds significance, echoing the profound mysteries of the Catholic faith. To understand these sacred objects is to delve into a deeper comprehension of God's ineffable presence and the narrative of salvation history. This exploration invites us to recognize in the objects of our worship not mere instruments, but symbols laden with divine significance, illuminating the path toward a more intimate encounter with the Divine.

The chalice, made of precious metal, holds not just wine but the Blood of Christ, a reminder of the ultimate sacrifice for humanity's redemption. Its polished surface reflects the community it serves, a visual testament to the unity and diversity of the Church, the body of Christ. When the priest raises the chalice, it becomes a beacon of hope, its gleam piercing the shadows of doubt and despair, affirming the victory of light over darkness.

The paten, often overshadowed by its companion, the chalice, carries the Bread of Life, soon to be consecrated as the Body of Christ. Its simplicity and purity of form underscore the humility of Christ, who became bread for the world. This humble vessel, therefore, becomes a profound symbol of God's generosity, inviting the faithful to partake in the Eucharist with a humble and open heart.

Altar candles, flickering with living flame, stand sentinel on either side of the altar, their light a symbol of Christ as the Light of the World. These candles, made of beeswax, speak of purity and sacrifice—the work of the bees a metaphor for the Christian community, laboring together for the sweetness of life found in God. As the light pierces the darkness of the sanctuary, it reminds the faithful of Christ's resurrected life, a beacon of hope in a shadowed world.

The processional cross, which leads the faithful into the sacred mysteries of the Mass, is a standard bearing the emblem of our salvation. It is both a declaration of victory over death and a call to carry our own crosses with dignity and courage. The cross, adorned and revered, is not merely an object of devotion but a lesson in love's transformative power.

The priest's vestments, rich in color and symbolism, envelop the celebration of the liturgy in beauty and reverence. Each piece, from the stole symbolizing authority and service to the chasuble embodying love and sacrifice, articulates aspects of Christ's ministry and the nature of the Church. Through these garments, the liturgical colors ebb and flow with the seasons, narrating the life of Christ and the journey of faith through the liturgical year.

The altar, the focal point of the liturgical space, stands as both tomb and table, where the sacrifices of the past and the banquet of the present converge in the mystery of the Eucharist. It invites the assembly to gather around for the sacrificial feast, uniting heaven and earth in the celebration of the Mass, a cornerstone of faith where the divine and human meet.

The incense, with its ascending smoke, symbolizes prayers rising to the heavens, carrying with it the hopes, sorrows, and joys of the faithful. Its sweet fragrance purifies the space, setting apart the mundane from the sacred, and envelops the congregation in a sensory reminder of the holiness of God's presence.

Fonts of holy water, placed at entrances, recall the baptismal promises and the cleansing power of baptism, which initiates the faithful into the mystery of Christ's death and resurrection. This act of blessing oneself with holy water, a simple yet profound gesture, serves as a daily renewal of faith, a reminder of one's identity as a beloved child of God.

The lectionary and the book of the Gospels, containing the Word of God, are not mere texts but the living voice of God speaking to His people. Their proclamation from the ambo transforms the liturgical assembly, making present Christ's teachings and inviting a response of faith. These sacred texts, adorned and venerated, are a testament to the power of God's Word to shape hearts and minds.

The sanctuary lamp, burning steadily beside the tabernacle, silently proclaims the real presence of Christ in the Eucharist. Its unwavering light, a comforting reminder of God's constant presence, calls the faithful to a moment of quiet prayer and adoration, a beacon of divine love in the midst of life's trials.

The tabernacle, veiled and revered, houses the consecrated Eucharist, the source and summit of Christian life. Its design and placement speak of the mystery it contains—God's immense love made manifest in a small host. The tabernacle stands as a profound symbol of God dwelling among His people, a sacred invitation to communion with the Divine.

Stations of the Cross, arrayed along the church walls, invite the faithful on a pilgrimage of reflection and penance, following the footsteps of Christ to Calvary. Each station, a snapshot of the Passion, serves as a mirror reflecting the trials and tribulations of human life, guiding the faithful to find comfort and courage in the sufferings of Christ.

The paschal candle, towering and inscribed with symbols of Christ's victory over death, burns brightly during the Easter season and at baptisms and funerals. It is a potent symbol of Christ, the Light of the World, who illuminates the path through death to life everlasting. Through this candle, the faithful are reminded that in Christ, death is not an end but a beginning, an entryway into eternal life.

In every liturgical object, there is an invitation to enter more deeply into the mystery it signifies. These objects, imbued with spiritual meaning, serve not only to beautify the liturgical celebration but to facilitate an encounter with the living God. They are silent teachers, guiding the faithful toward a fuller participation in the sacramental life and a deeper understanding of the divine mysteries.

In conclusion, the symbolism imbued in liturgical objects serves as a bridge between the physical and the spiritual, between the community of believers and the divine mysteries they celebrate. Through these sacred symbols, the Church communicates the depth of its faith, inviting every heart to ascend toward the transcendent, toward a deeper communion with the Divine. In the artistry and symbolism of these liturgical elements, the faithful find a reflection of God's beauty, a glimpse of the eternal banquet to which all are called.

Chapter 18: Folk Art and Popular Devotions

Within the rich tapestry of Catholic tradition, the strands of folk art
and popular devotions weave a compelling narrative of faith,
identity, and communal expression. As vibrant manifestations of
devotion, these artistic expressions serve not only as vehicles for
personal piety but also as profound communal experiences that
reinforce the catholicity - the universality - of the Church. Folk art,
in its myriad forms, embodies the nuanced interplay between
culture, faith, and the human impulse to create objects of beauty that
reflect the divine.

The Virgin of Guadalupe stands as a seminal icon in the realm of
folk art and popular devotion, transcending geographic and cultural
boundaries to become a global emblem of maternal comfort and
protection. This image not only exemplifies the power of visual art
to encapsulate complex theological truths but also highlights the role
of folk art as a medium for expressing deeply felt devotions in a
manner that is accessible and emotionally resonant for the faithful.

At its core, folk art in the Catholic tradition is an expression of the
vernacular - the language of the people. It is through these
grassroots creations that the faithful can engage with sacred
mysteries using the materials, symbols, and techniques that are
familiar and meaningful within their own cultural context. This
localization of the sacred forms a bridge between the heavenly and

the earthly, allowing individuals to encounter God in the midst of their daily lives.

Popular devotions, encompassing practices such as novenas, processions, and the veneration of relics and images, function as tangible expressions of faith that foster a sense of belonging and community among participants. These devotions, deeply embedded in local cultures, offer the faithful avenues for expressing love, gratitude, and petition to God, often through the intercession of the saints. The communal aspect of these practices cannot be overstated; it is in the shared experience of prayer and devotion that the Church reveals its true character as the Body of Christ.

Moreover, the role of folk art and popular devotions in evangelization and catechesis should not be overlooked. Through these accessible and relatable forms, the core tenets of Catholic faith can be communicated and internalized, often more effectively than through formal theological discourse. The stories of faith, hope, and charity depicted in folk art, and the rituals of devotion practiced by communities, serve to educate and inspire both the faithful and those exploring the faith.

Yet, the significance of folk art and popular devotions extends beyond their educational and evangelizing functions. These expressions of faith are acts of co-creation with the Divine, reflecting humanity's innate desire to contribute to the unfolding story of salvation. In crafting an image or engaging in a procession, the faithful participate in a creative act that mirrors God's creative work. It is a profound cooperation with grace, where the ordinary materials of the world are transformed into extraordinary vehicles of spiritual truth.

This dynamic interplay between creation, culture, and faith within folk art and popular devotions illuminates the theological concept of sacramentality. Through these tangible expressions, the spiritual reality they signify is made present and accessible. As such, folk art and popular devotions are sacramentals in their own right, beckoning the faithful to a deeper engagement with the mysteries of faith.

In the final analysis, folk art and popular devotions represent the heart's cry of the faithful, rendered in color, form, and ritual. They are the fruits of a faith that is lived and experienced in the everyday, a testament to the indissoluble bond between God and humanity. As channels of grace, they draw the faithful closer to the Divine, serving as both mirror and window to the soul's deepest longings and its eternal destiny.

Thus, in contemplating the rich heritage of folk art and popular devotions within the Catholic tradition, one is drawn into a deeper appreciation of the Church's mission to sanctify the world. Through these humble yet profound expressions of faith, the Spirit moves, drawing all towards the fullness of life in God.

In sum, folk art and popular devotions are not mere embellishments to the fabric of Catholic faith; rather, they are integral threads that contribute to the Church's vibrant and living tapestry. They stand as testaments to the power of beauty and tradition to convey truth, foster unity, and inspire devotion. As the Church looks to the future, the nourishment of these expressions, rooted in the past yet ever new, will continue to be essential in the sacred quest to illuminate God's grace in the world.

The Virgin of Guadalupe and Other Devotions

In the realm of Catholic folk art and popular devotions, the Virgin of Guadalupe holds a place of singular eminence, her image serving as a lodestar guiding the faithful towards the divine. The tradition surrounding the Virgin of Guadalupe is not merely an art form; it is a fervent expression of faith, interweaving the sacred with the secular, the celestial with the commonplace. This portrayal, emblematic of the Virgin Mary's apparition to Juan Diego on the hill of Tepeyac in 1531, anchors a vast constellation of devotional practices and artistic expressions that resonate deeply within the Catholic community.

Folk art, in its most profound essence, is a testament to the interplay between divine inspiration and human creativity. Artists, often self-taught, imbue everyday materials with a sacred significance, crafting tangible manifestations of their inner spiritual visions. These creations, ranging from simple votive offerings to intricate pictorial representations, serve as conduits of grace, uniting the creator and beholder in a shared experience of the transcendent.

Central to this communion is the figure of the Virgin of Guadalupe, whose image, rendered with an array of materials and techniques, symbolizes an inexhaustible wellspring of consolation and hope. Through her, artisans and devotees alike explore the depths of their faith, expressing their devotion in a multitude of forms that transcend linguistic and cultural boundaries. The Virgin's image, whether adorning the humblest of homes or the grandest of cathedrals, acts as a beacon of light, guiding the faithful through the vicissitudes of life towards the promise of divine love.

Moreover, the Virgin of Guadalupe embodies the synthesis of indigenous and Spanish influences, mirroring the broader cultural mestizaje that characterizes much of Latin America's religious landscape. This amalgamation is not merely aesthetic; it signifies a profound reconciliation of disparate elements, crafting a shared identity rooted in faith. Artists, drawing on this rich tapestry of symbols and traditions, create works that are at once deeply personal and universally resonant, bridging the gap between heaven and earth.

At the heart of this artistic and devotional phenomenon lies the concept of offering. Each work, no matter its form or scale, is an act of surrender, a tangible expression of the artist's love and reverence for the divine. This notion of offering extends beyond the confines of the art world, permeating everyday acts of devotion and shaping the very fabric of Catholic life. Through prayer, pilgrimage, and the creation of sacred art, believers participate in an ongoing dialogue with the divine, a conversation that is both intimate and infinite.

The Virgin's presence in the realm of folk art and popular devotions also serves as a testament to the enduring power of story and symbol in the Catholic imagination. Her image, accompanied by the narrative of her appearances and miracles, functions as a catalyst for faith, inspiring countless individuals to deepen their spiritual journey. This interplay between story and symbol, rooted in the Virgin's enduring appeal, highlights the dynamic nature of Catholic devotion, which continually evolves while remaining anchored to the bedrock of tradition.

In examining the Virgin of Guadalupe and the myriad devotions that she inspires, one cannot overlook the communal aspect these practices foster. Gatherings for prayer, processions, and the creation and veneration of sacred images serve to knit the faithful together, creating a sense of belonging and shared purpose. This communal dimension is crucial, for it reflects the Church's teaching on the Mystical Body of Christ, emphasizing the interconnectedness of all members of the faithful.

Finally, the study of the Virgin of Guadalupe and other devotions within the framework of folk art opens new avenues for understanding the role of beauty in the spiritual life. The creation and veneration of these works reveal an intrinsic human desire for beauty, which, in its highest form, leads the soul towards the ultimate source of all beauty, God Himself. In this light, folk art and popular devotions are not mere adjuncts to the faith; they are vital expressions of the Church's mission to evangelize through beauty, drawing all people into the embrace of divine love.

In conclusion, the Virgin of Guadalupe and the rich tapestry of devotions that surround her illustrate the profound capacity of art to serve as a bridge to the divine. Through these expressions of faith, the faithful are invited to encounter God in the midst of their daily lives, transforming the ordinary into the extraordinary, the temporal into the eternal. In this sacred dialogue, art becomes not only a reflection of divine beauty but also a means of participating in the divine life, a testament to the limitless creativity bestowed upon humanity by the Creator.

The Role of Folk Art in Expressing Faith Amidst the tapestry of Catholic tradition and devotion, folk art emerges as a vibrant thread, interwoven with the daily lives and spiritual practices of the faithful. This expression of art, born from the heart of the community, serves not only as a reflection of cultural identity but as a profound declaration of faith. It is within this nexus of creativity and belief that folk art finds its most authentic purpose, acting as a conduit for spiritual expression and communion with the divine.

Folk art, in its essence, is the art of the people. It springs forth from the well of collective memory and experience, passed down through generations, each adding their own voice to a chorus that spans the ages. It is a manifestation of the innate human desire to create, to beautify one's environment, and to give form to faith. This form of art transcends mere aesthetic appeal, embedding itself in the traditions and rituals of the community, and in doing so, serves a dual role as a bearer of tradition and a vehicle for catechesis.

The Catholic Church, with its rich tapestry of rites and devotions, has long recognized the power of art to touch the human soul and lift it towards the divine. The Second Vatican Council's document "Sacrosanctum Concilium" acknowledges the importance of sacred art in leading the faithful to the mystery of the divine, highlighting the Church's duty to foster and safeguard such expressions of faith (Vatican II, 1963). Folk art, in its various forms, embodies this call, acting as a tangible link between the celestial and the terrestrial, between God and His people.

In the realm of folk art, the representation of saints and sacred events occupies a prominent place. These images serve not only as objects of veneration but as tools for education and reflection. Through the lens of folk art, stories of faith, courage, and sanctity are rendered accessible, making the lives of the saints and the mysteries of the faith tangible to every believer, regardless of their level of formal religious education.

The role of Marian devotion in Catholic folk art cannot be overstated. The Virgin Mary, revered as the Mother of God and the archetype of submission to divine will, appears frequently in this genre. Whether depicted in the intricate patterns of a woven tapestry or the simple strokes of a peasant's brush, the image of Mary serves as a beacon of faith, a reminder of the Church's maternal care for her children.

The significance of folk art also lies in its capacity to convey the sacred in the midst of the secular. Festivals, processions, and other public expressions of faith often incorporate elements of folk art, blending the spiritual with the cultural in a celebration of community identity anchored in a shared belief. It is within these communal gatherings that folk art takes on a performative aspect, becoming an act of worship in itself.

Moreover, the creation of folk art serves as a meditative practice, a form of prayer wherein the artist offers their work as a gift to God. Through the act of creation, the artist enters into a dialogue with the Creator, an intimate exchange where the boundaries between the divine and the human blur. This creative process reflects the broader Catholic understanding of co-creation with God, where human creativity participates in the divine creative act.

Despite its profound significance, folk art often operates on the margins of formal religious art. Its value, however, should not be underestimated. Folk art embodies the inculturation of faith, the process by which the Gospel takes root within a particular cultural context and flourishes. It exemplifies the Catholic Church's universal reach, adapting and integrating into diverse cultures while preserving the integrity of the Gospel message.

As the Church moves forward, navigating the challenges and opportunities of the modern world, the role of folk art in evangelization and catechesis remains vital. In an era marked by rapid change and increasing secularization, folk art stands as a testament to the enduring power of faith expressed through the creativity of the human heart.

The educational potential of folk art is also noteworthy. Beyond its role in catechesis, folk art can facilitate encounters with the divine for those outside the faith. Through its beauty and simplicity, folk art can speak to the universal human search for meaning, making it an invaluable tool for the New Evangelization, which seeks to repropose the Gospel in contemporary contexts (Pope Benedict XVI, 2010).

Ultimately, the significance of folk art in expressing faith lies in its ability to bridge the gap between the individual and the communal, the earthly and the heavenly. It is a form of art that belongs to the people, reflecting their joys, sorrows, and aspirations, all while pointing them towards the transcendent. In this way, folk art serves not only as an expression of faith but as a catalyst for the deepening of that faith.

The challenge for the Church today is to recognize and nurture the value of folk art within the liturgical and devotional life of the community. By doing so, the Church not only preserves a rich cultural heritage but also fosters a living faith that is continually renewed and expressed in the creative works of its people.

In conclusion, folk art holds a unique place within the tapestry of Catholic tradition and devotion. Through its simple yet profound expressions of faith, it serves as a reminder that art, in all its forms, is a gift from God, intended to draw us closer to Him. In the creation and veneration of folk art, the faithful participate in a sacred act of worship, one that transcends words and touches the heart. It is in this sacred act that the true role of folk art in expressing faith is fully realized.

Chapter 19: The Transformative Power of Sacred Music

The interplay between the divine and the human often unfolds in the melodious strains of sacred music, where the soul's ascent to God finds expression in harmonious sounds. This chapter delves into the profound impact of sacred music on the human heart and its role in the liturgy and personal devotion, exploring how it acts as both a vehicle for prayer and a manifestation of the divine within the temporal realm.

At the core of Catholic tradition, sacred music such as Gregorian chant and polyphony has served not merely as an accessory to worship but as an integral part of the liturgical experience. Historically, composers of faith, ranging from the medieval monks to Renaissance maestros like Palestrina, composed works that transcend time, carrying with them the theological depth and beauty of the faith. These compositions are not just music; they are catechesis, prayer, and theology rendered in sound (O'Malley, 2015).

The role of choirs and congregational singing in the liturgy cannot be overstated. The Second Vatican Council's document "Sacrosanctum Concilium" emphasizes the participatory nature of liturgical music, inviting the whole congregation to unite their voices in praise and worship. This communal aspect of sacred music underscores the communal nature of faith itself, pulling the faithful out of isolation and into the shared experience of God's presence.

What sets sacred music apart is its capacity to transform the ordinary into the extraordinary, to elevate the human experience into a dialogue with the divine. It creates a space where heaven and earth seem to converge, and the boundaries between the temporal and the eternal blur. In the strains of a beautifully executed Kyrie or the soaring notes of a Sanctus, the faithful encounter the mystery and majesty of God in a way that words alone cannot convey.

Moreover, composers of faith have historically imbued their works with theological insights and spiritual depth. From Bach's cantatas, inscribed with dedications "Soli Deo Gloria" (To God Alone the Glory), to the profound simplicity of Gounod's Ave Maria, the repertoire of sacred music serves as a testament to the composers' own spiritual journeys and their attempts to articulate the inarticulable: the experience of the divine.

However, the transformative power of sacred music is not limited to the confines of the church or the sanctity of the liturgy. Its influence extends into the personal sphere, offering a source of comfort, inspiration, and spiritual nourishment. Many find in sacred music a companion in their own spiritual journey, a means of drawing closer to God amidst the trials of everyday life.

Yet, the true beauty of sacred music lies not in its aesthetic appeal but in its capacity to speak directly to the soul. It bypasses the intellect and the barriers we construct around our hearts, speaking a universal language of the spirit. In its purest form, sacred music is prayer, an outpouring of the human heart towards the divine, an echo of the eternal call and response between God and humanity.

In conclusion, the transformative power of sacred music lies in its ability to bridge the gap between the human and the divine, to elevate the soul and draw it into closer communion with God. It enriches the liturgy, deepens personal devotion, and fosters a sense of community among the faithful. As both an expression of faith and a means of encountering the divine, sacred music remains an indispensable treasure of the Church, a wellspring of spiritual vitality and a beacon of the transcendent amidst the temporal.

The Role of Choirs and Congregational Singing

In the grand tapestry of sacred music, choirs and congregational singing emerge as threads which bind the fabric of Catholic worship and tradition. These musical elements do not merely add aesthetic value to the liturgy; they serve a profounder purpose, intertwining with the essence of communal prayer and the sacramental life of the Church. At the heart of their role lies the capacity to transform the worship space into a resonant vessel of divine communion, a space where heaven and earth converge through the medium of sound.

Choirs, with their disciplined harmonies and layered voices, act as the custodians of the Church's musical heritage. Their function extends beyond performance; they are educators, role models, and leaders in worship. When a choir lifts its voice in a Gregorian chant or a polyphonic masterpiece, it invites the congregation into a historical continuum of faith, echoing the prayers of generations past. This continuity fosters a sense of unity and shared identity, grounding the present in the rich soil of tradition.

Similarly, congregational singing democratizes the act of worship, embracing the biblical injunction to "sing psalms, hymns, and spiritual songs" (Ephesians 5:19). When the voices of the congregation rise in unity, distinctions of class, age, and ability dissolve, encapsulating the ideal of the Church as the Body of Christ. This participatory approach to music emphasizes that each believer holds a place in the chorus of faith, contributing their voice to the collective expression of love and adoration for God.

The interplay between choirs and congregational singing also illustrates the Church's understanding of beauty as a vehicle for transcendence. Sacred music, in its intrinsic beauty, possesses the power to elevate the mind and heart, directing them towards the divine. In this capacity, music becomes an instrument of catechesis, teaching through beauty and stirring the soul towards contemplation of the mysteries of faith.

The role of these musical elements in the liturgy also underscores the incarnational aspect of Catholic worship. Just as the Word became flesh and dwelt among us (John 1:14), so too does sacred music become a tangible manifestation of the Word. Through choirs and congregational song, the abstract becomes concrete, and the divine message is communicated in a form that touches not only the ear but also the heart.

Moreover, the act of singing together in worship embodies the communal aspect of the Church's mission. In a world where individualism often prevails, choirs and congregational singing serve as reminders of our interconnectedness in the Body of Christ. Through shared melodies and rhythms, worshippers experience a visceral sense of solidarity, reinforcing the social dimension of liturgical participation.

It is important to acknowledge that the transformative power of sacred music, as mediated through choirs and congregational singing, extends beyond the confines of the Mass. These musical expressions carry forth into the daily lives of believers, echoing in their hearts and minds, and influencing the way they live out their faith in the world. In this way, sacred music serves as a continuous source of spiritual nourishment and inspiration.

In conclusion, the roles of choirs and congregational singing within the framework of Catholic worship are multifaceted and profound. They are not merely decorative elements but are integral to the liturgical life of the Church, fostering a sense of community, continuity with tradition, and a deepened experience of the sacred. Through these musical expressions, worshippers are invited to partake in the transformative power of sacred music, encountering the divine in the most resonant chambers of their souls.

Composers of Faith As we delve into the illustrious realm of sacred music within the Catholic tradition, it is imperative to examine the role of those illustrious souls whose compositions have not merely filled the naves and apses of countless churches but have also elevated the hearts and minds of the faithful towards the Divine. Music, in its transcendent purity and harmonic complexity, serves not only as an art form but as a profound medium of spiritual communion and theological expression, bridging the earthly with the heavenly.

In the grand tapestry of Catholic music, the composers stand as intermediaries, channeling through their creative faculties the whispers of the divine spirit. Their craft goes beyond mere musical composition; it is an act of faith, a devout offering to the glory of God. Each note penned and every melody conceived is an articulation of spiritual longing, a reflection of the interior life of the composer devoted to the divine mystery.

From the hallowed grounds of monastic communities to the majestic cathedrals of Europe, music has served as a central pillar of Catholic worship and devotion. The liturgical calendar, with its seasons and feasts, finds in music a profound expression of its theological themes and spiritual moods. Composers, deeply versed in the rituals and texts of the Church, crafted works that not only enhanced the liturgy but also educated and moved the faithful in their spiritual journey.

The tradition of Catholic sacred music is notably marked by the contributions of figures such as Palestrina, whose polyphonic masses and motets have earned him a place as a master of Renaissance church music. His works, characterized by clarity, balance, and serenity, embody a profound spiritual aesthetic that has inspired generations of composers and faithful alike. Palestrina's compositions, deeply rooted in the liturgical and doctrinal heritage of the Church, reflect an understanding of music's role as a medium of divine worship and a vehicle for spiritual contemplation.

In the Baroque period, composers like Vivaldi and Bach, though differing in their religious affiliations, contributed significantly to the repository of sacred music, with Bach's compositions, in particular, exemplifying the Lutheran tradition's influence on Catholic sacred music. Bach's cantatas and passions, rich in theological depth and expressive intensity, remain pivotal in the sacred music tradition, illustrating the universality and ecumenical reach of music as a language of faith.

Moving into the classical and romantic eras, Mozart and Beethoven, among others, brought to sacred music a new breadth of emotional expressiveness and structural complexity. Mozart's masses and Requiem, replete with lyrical beauty and dramatic contrasts, manifest a luminous spiritual vision, while Beethoven's Missa Solemnis stands as a monumental expression of faith, a testament to the transcendental power of music to communicate the ineffable.

In the contemporary landscape, composers such as John Tavener and Arvo Pärt have sought to reconcile the ancient with the modern, infusing their works with a mystic solemnity that speaks to the spiritual yearnings of today's world. Tavener's compositions, often inspired by Eastern Christian liturgical traditions, and Pärt's tintinnabuli style reflect a minimalist yet profoundly spiritual approach to composition, inviting the listener into a space of contemplative silence and divine encounter.

The journey of faith is inherently musical, a symphony of divine grace played out in the lives of the faithful. Composers, in their unique role as creators of sacred music, participate in this divine economy of salvation, their works serving as bridges between the temporal and the eternal. Through the beauty and spiritual depth of their compositions, they invite the faithful to partake in the mystery of faith, leading hearts and minds into the presence of the Living God.

The ecclesial context provides these composers not only with inspiration but also with a framework within which their music acquires liturgical and sacramental significance. In the celebration of the Mass and the Liturgy of the Hours, sacred music finds its fullest expression and purpose, elevating the liturgical texts and rites, and facilitating the participation of the people in the sacred mysteries.

It is also worth noting the pedagogical function of sacred music in the life of the Church. Through hymns, antiphons, and choral works, the faithful are catechized, immersed in the theological virtues of faith, hope, and charity. Composers, aware of the educational power of music, have often crafted works that elucidate doctrinal truths, biblical narratives, and the lives of the saints, thereby contributing to the spiritual formation of the faithful.

The vocation of the composer of faith is thus a profound calling, requiring not only musical talent and creativity but also a deep spiritual life and commitment to the Church's liturgical and doctrinal heritage. In their pursuit of artistic excellence, these composers are guided by the principles of truth, goodness, and beauty, seeking to reflect in their works the splendor of the Creator.

In conclusion, the composers of faith stand as luminaries in the Church's artistic heritage, their works bearing witness to the power of music as a form of prayer and a means of encountering the Divine. Through their contributions, the tradition of sacred music continues to flourish, enriching the Church's liturgical life and inspiring the faithful in their spiritual journey towards the beatific vision.

Chapter 20: Drama and Dance: Movement as Prayer

In the vast panorama of Catholic art, drama and dance occupy a distinctive place, serving as channels for divine grace through the poetry of movement and narrative. This chapter delves into the sacred essence of these art forms, exploring their historical evolution and profound capacity to articulate the ineffable truths of our faith. At the heart of this exploration is the recognition that both drama and dance, in their most elevated forms, transcend mere entertainment to become acts of prayer and profound expressions of the human soul's longing for the divine.

The tradition of religious plays, deeply rooted in the liturgical life of the church, offers a poignant illustration of drama as a form of prayer. From the medieval mystery plays that brought biblical stories to vibrant life for those outside the church walls to the contemporary passion plays that continue to inspire and unify communities, drama has served as a living catechism. These performances, steeped in the narratives of salvation history, invite both actors and audience into a deeper meditation on the mysteries of faith, transforming the stage into an altar of sorts—a place where heaven and earth meet.

Parallel to the narrative power of drama is the symbolic potency of sacred dance. Historically marginalized within certain segments of the church, sacred dance has nonetheless found a place within the tapestry of Catholic worship, particularly in the Eastern rites and certain religious communities. This art form embodies prayer through the harmonious movement of the body, creating a visible doxology that echoes the celestial liturgy. Sacred dance, with its roots entwined with the earliest human expressions of joy and worship, invites the faithful into a participatory experience of the divine, transcending words to touch the soul directly.

Indeed, when drama and dance are infused with the intention of glorifying God, they become powerful instruments of evangelization and education. In a culture increasingly dominated by visual and kinetic forms of communication, these art forms can articulate the truths of the Gospel in a language that is at once ancient and urgently contemporary. They remind us that our bodies, as well as our voices and intellects, are capable of proclaiming and encountering the divine.

Yet, integrating drama and dance into the life of the church requires discernment and a deep respect for the sacred traditions and liturgical norms that guide Catholic worship. The Second Vatican Council's document on the sacred liturgy, Sacrosanctum Concilium, while opening the door to liturgical adaptation for the sake of inculturation, also underscores the importance of ensuring that such expressions truly serve to edify the faithful and elevate the worship of God.

This sacred balance is exemplified in the work of liturgical dance ensembles that interpret biblical narratives and themes of faith through movement, carefully woven into the liturgical celebrations in a manner that enhances rather than distracts from the spirit of prayer. Similarly, religious drama, when thoughtfully integrated into parish life or educational programs, can become a profound means of catechesis, bringing the stories of scripture and the saints to life in a way that is both engaging and transformative.

As we reflect on the role of drama and dance within the Catholic imagination, we are reminded that these art forms, like all true art, have the potential to embody the beauty and truth of our faith. They testify to the incarnation—the Word made flesh—and invite us to consider our own bodies as instruments of praise and vehicles of God's grace. In this light, the movement of the dancer and the voice of the actor join the chorus of creation that sings of the glory of God.

Thus, drama and dance, as expressions of prayer, call us to a deeper awareness of the sacredness of our physical existence and the potential of human creativity to touch the divine. They challenge us to reconsider our understanding of worship, expanding it to include the full range of human expression and reminding us that every gesture of our being can be an offering to God.

In conclusion, drama and dance in their sacred forms invite us into a profound communion with the divine, a communion that is both deeply personal and inherently communal. As movements of prayer, they embody the joy, sorrow, hope, and longing that define our journey of faith, inviting us to move, body and soul, in harmony with the eternal dance of divine love.

"For in him we live and move and have our being" (Acts 17:28). In the sacred expressions of drama and dance, we find a reflection of this profound truth, an invitation to experience and embody the presence of God through the grace-filled movements of our lives.

The Tradition of Religious Plays

The tradition of religious plays, within the broad tapestry of Catholic art and culture, occupies a unique and vital role. This genre, evolved from the early medieval liturgical dramas to the grand Passion plays of the modern era, illustrates a profound synthesis of faith, artistry, and community. At its core, the tradition of religious plays serves not merely as entertainment but as a profound meditative act, a dynamic prayer that seeks to unify the divine narrative with human experience.

The genesis of religious plays can be traced back to the medieval period, a time when the church sought to educate and engage a largely illiterate populace. These early dramas were simple renditions of Biblical stories, particularly the life, death, and resurrection of Christ, intended to make the sacred narratives accessible to all. It was here, within the echoing halls of cathedrals and the town squares, that the seeds of religious theater were sown, intertwining scriptural teachings with the vibrancy of performance.

As these plays evolved, they began to extend beyond the confines of church walls, blooming in complexity and scope. The Passion plays, most notably the ones performed in cities like Oberammergau, stand as a testament to this evolution. These performances, often running for several hours, weave together the narratives of Christ's suffering, death, and resurrection with unparalleled depth and devotion. The Oberammergau Passion Play, for instance, has been performed once every decade since 1634, epitomizing the endurance and communal spirit of religious theater.

This expansion saw the inclusion of a wide array of biblical and apocryphal stories, which were adapted to fit the stage. The performances became a staple of community life, serving not only as spiritual observances but also as occasions for social gathering. Through the medium of theater, the stories of saints, martyrs, and biblical heroes were brought to vivid life, reaching audiences in a manner that was both emotionally compelling and spiritually uplifting.

Moreover, religious plays have been instrumental in bridging cultural and linguistic divides. In many parts of the world, these plays were adapted to local languages and contexts, thus becoming a powerful tool for evangelization and cultural exchange. They offered a shared space where faith and art could intersect, creating a universal language that transcends geographical and cultural boundaries.

In the contemporary era, the tradition of religious plays continues to thrive, adapting to new challenges and opportunities presented by modernity. Across the globe, churches, schools, and community groups stage performances that endeavor to connect with audiences in a language they understand, employing modern technology and innovative stagecraft to enrich the narrative and sensory experience of the sacred dramas. This adaptability highlights the enduring relevance of religious theater as a means of spiritual reflection and communal engagement.

At its heart, the tradition of religious plays embodies the Catholic Church's understanding of beauty as a path to God. Through the powerful medium of drama, audiences are invited to ponder the mysteries of faith, to empathize with the spiritual journeys of biblical characters, and to reflect on their own relationship with the divine. It is here, amidst the confluence of sacred text and human expression, that the viewer is afforded a glimpse into the profound truths of the Christian faith.

Yet, the significance of religious plays extends beyond their immediate impact on audiences. These dramas serve as a vivid reminder of the church's commitment to nurturing creativity within the context of faith. They stand as a testament to the belief that art, in all its forms, is not merely decorative but fundamentally transformative, capable of conveying spiritual truths and inspiring a deeper engagement with the divine.

In conclusion, the tradition of religious plays offers a fascinating insight into the Catholic imagination, where the enactment of divine narratives serves as both an act of worship and a profound communal experience. As this tradition continues to evolve, it remains a vibrant testament to the enduring power of faith, art, and community to inspire, educate, and transform.

Sacred Dance as Liturgical Expression Within the rich tapestry of Catholic art and liturgy, the sacred dance emerges as a harmonious symphony of bodily movement, elevating the soul towards the divine. It's an art form that transcends mere aesthetic appreciation, embodying theological truth and spiritual yearning. Sacred dance in the Catholic tradition is not merely a performance, but a profound liturgical expression that participates in the heavenly liturgy, mirroring the angels and saints in their eternal worship of God.

In the early Church, dance was viewed as an integral part of spiritual life and communal worship. Historical accounts and theological treatises suggest that dance accompanied liturgical celebrations, particularly in the Eastern traditions of the Church. It was seen as a manifestation of joy and a visible sign of the inner movement of the soul towards God. This perspective on dance is rooted in a theology that appreciates the human body as a gift from God, capable of expressing divine truths and participating in the salvific mystery of Christ.

The sacredness of dance in liturgical settings has been subject to various interpretations and regulations throughout Church history. In the Western Church, formal liturgical dance has been less prevalent, often restricted by concerns over reverence in liturgical celebrations. However, this has not stifled the creative spirit of those who seek to express their faith through movement. The Second Vatican Council's call for the active participation of the faithful and the incorporation of diverse cultural expressions into liturgy opened new pathways for the exploration of dance as a form of worship.

Efforts to integrate dance into liturgical celebrations have been cautious yet hopeful. Sacred dance, when appropriately incorporated, enhances the liturgical experience by drawing participants deeper into the mystery being celebrated. It serves as a powerful medium for the expression of penitence, celebration, and supplication. The key is ensuring that the dance serves the liturgy, complementing the liturgical action rather than drawing attention away from it.

Sacred dance's potential for catechesis and evangelization illuminates another aspect of its importance. Through symbolic gestures and movements, the dance narrates the Christian mystery, conveying theological truths in a way that words alone cannot. It breaks the boundaries of language, reaching out to the human heart directly through the beauty of form and movement. This evangelizing aspect aligns with the Church's mission to communicate the Gospel in diverse and impactful ways.

Diverse cultural expressions of dance within the Church demonstrate the universality of Catholicism. African liturgies, for instance, often incorporate movement and dance in ways that are deeply integrated into the communal worship experience. Similarly, in parts of Asia and the Pacific, dance forms a critical part of the expression of faith and cultural identity. These expressions of sacred dance highlight the Church's capacity to embrace and sanctify cultural diversity.

For sacred dance to truly serve its liturgical and evangelizing purpose, it must adhere to certain principles. It should respect the sacredness of the liturgical space and the dignity of the human person. The movements should express humility, reverence, and joy, reflecting the interior disposition of the dancer towards God. Moreover, the incorporation of sacred dance into liturgy demands discernment and pastoral sensitivity to ensure that it enhances, rather than detracts from, the liturgical celebration.

Educational programs and workshops on sacred dance have emerged, fostering a deeper understanding of its role and significance in liturgy and prayer. These programs aim to cultivate an appreciation for the sacredness of the body and movement, encouraging participants to explore dance as a form of prayer and worship. They highlight the importance of intentionality and preparation, showing that sacred dance is not merely a performance but an act of worship that requires spiritual readiness.

The theological foundation of sacred dance is found in the Incarnation, the Word made flesh. This mystery reveals the sanctity of the human body and its capacity to mediate divine grace. Sacred dance, as a liturgical expression, embodies this profound truth, inviting the faithful to experience God's presence through the sanctified movement of the body.

Critics of sacred dance raise legitimate concerns regarding the potential for distraction and irreverence in the liturgical context. These concerns underline the need for careful discernment in the selection and choreography of the dance. When done with respect for liturgical norms and sensitivity to the local culture and tradition, sacred dance can be a beautiful and enriching addition to worship, enhancing its expressive and catechetical dimensions.

Scholars like Lang (2012) emphasize the transformative power of sacred dance, noting its capacity to engage the faithful in a holistic worship experience that involves body, soul, and spirit. The integration of sacred dance into liturgy, Lang argues, can facilitate a deeper encounter with the divine, fostering a sense of unity and communal participation in the sacred mysteries.

Despite the challenges and controversies surrounding sacred dance, its potential as a liturgical expression cannot be underestimated. Its beauty and expressiveness can open hearts to the transcendent, fostering a deeper engagement with the liturgical action and enriching the Church's worship with the fullness of human expression. As the Church continues to explore and embrace diverse forms of art within liturgy, sacred dance stands as a testament to the enduring power of beauty to draw souls closer to God.

In conclusion, sacred dance as liturgical expression represents a fusion of tradition and innovation, symbolizing the Church's ongoing journey towards a fuller understanding of worship. It encapsulates the dynamic interaction between divine grace and human creativity, embodying the call to lift hearts and minds to God through every available means. As such, sacred dance remains a vibrant and poignant expression of faith, a dance of the soul that mirrors the heavenly liturgy and anticipates the joy of the eternal banquet.

Chapter 21: Film, Media, and Catholic Storytelling

In the panorama of Catholic art, the adaptation of sacred narratives and theological insights into film and media represents a fascinating and challenging frontier. This chapter explores the evolution and impact of Catholic storytelling through these contemporary mediums, which serve as canvases for faith in the modern era. Much as stained glass windows once narrated the Christian mysteries to the illiterate, today's films and digital media extend a similar invitation to a global audience, beckoning them into the depth of Catholic thought and culture.

The incursion of Catholicism into film and media is not merely an extension of traditional art forms but signifies a profound engagement with the modern world. Cinema, with its unique capability to weave visuals, music, and narrative into a singular, immersive experience, offers an unparalleled opportunity to convey complex theological concepts and the subtleties of spiritual life. The medium's ability to encompass the breadth of human experience - from suffering and redemption to love and sacrifice - mirrors the Catholic Church's own narrative.

Nevertheless, the challenges of presenting Catholicism within the contemporary media landscape are manifold. The tension between the transcendent and the immanent, the sacred and the profane, often results in divergent portrayals that can either uplift the soul or mislead it. It's a delicate balance to maintain authenticity of faith while ensuring the narrative's relevance and accessibility to modern audiences. The risk of diluting complex theological truths to fit the narrative constraints of film, or alternatively, of alienating viewers with doctrinal rigorism, looms large in the Catholic filmmaker's endeavour.

Despite these challenges, there have been notable successes in Catholic storytelling through film and media that offer a window into the potential of this endeavor. These works have demonstrated that it is indeed possible to craft narratives that resonate with both Catholics and the broader public, fostering a deeper appreciation and understanding of Catholicism. They serve as beacons of light, illustrating the profound impact that faith-informed media can have on individual hearts and minds, as well as on culture at large.

Central to the effectiveness of Catholic storytelling in film and media is its sacramental vision of reality. This perspective sees the material world as a vessel for the divine, where ordinary elements - bread, wine, water - become conduits of grace. When filmmakers imbue their work with this sacramental sensibility, even the most mundane of stories can become radiant with the presence of the divine. It is this ability to imbue the temporal with the echo of the eternal that sets Catholic storytelling apart in the modern media landscape.

The integration of Catholic themes into film and media also serves an evangelical purpose. In an age where traditional forms of evangelization may no longer resonate as they once did, media becomes a vital arena for the Church's mission. Films and digital content that authentically and compellingly explore the Catholic faith can open new doors for dialogue, invite introspection, and even inspire conversion. They can become the initial touchpoint for encounters with the divine, the catalyst for deeper exploration into the faith.

However, achieving a successful integration of faith and film necessitates a deep understanding of both scripture and cinematic language. The Catholic storyteller must be both a theologian and an artist, capable of translating the depth of Catholic tradition into the visual and narrative grammar of film. This requires a discerning use of symbol, metaphor, and allegory, tools that bridge the gap between the seen and the unseen, the temporal and the eternal.

As we look to the future of Catholic storytelling in film and media, it's clear that continued creativity, innovation, and theological fidelity are essential. The Church finds itself at a crossroads of tradition and modernity, called to proclaim the timeless truth of the Gospel in the ever-evolving language of media. The journey ahead is fraught with challenges, but it's also ripe with opportunity. For in every frame, every scene, and every narrative lies the potential to reveal the face of God to a world in dire need of his presence.

In this exploration, it's evident that film and media are not mere secular inventions but can be harnessed as powerful tools for spiritual reflection and catechesis. The growing body of Catholic film and digital media stands as a testament to the Church's ongoing conversation with the modern world, a dialogue grounded in the hope of transcending the mundane to touch the divine. As Catholic storytellers continue to navigate this complex landscape, their work illuminates the path for a Church seeking to evangelize with beauty and truth in the third millennium.

Cinema as a Canvas for Faith

In exploring the intersection of film, media, and Catholic storytelling, one must recognize cinema's potent capacity as a canvas for faith. The moving image, with its unique blend of visual artistry, narrative, and sound, offers a compelling medium through which the Catholic imagination can articulate the mysteries of faith, grace, and human experience. The art of filmmaking, when approached with a sacramental vision, becomes not merely entertainment but a profound means of encountering truth.

The historical evolution of cinema has witnessed the emergence of films that, intentionally or not, echo the tenets of the Catholic faith. These narratives, whether grounded in biblical stories, the lives of saints, or moral dilemmas reflective of Catholic teaching, contribute to a rich tapestry that portrays the human quest for meaning, redemption, and communion with the Divine.

Central to Catholic thought is the Incarnation, the Word made flesh. In a manner akin to this mystery, film incarnates ideas, bringing abstract concepts into a tangible form. This analogy elucidates cinema's power to make the invisible visible, to clothe spiritual truths in the materiality of image and sound. Through this lens, the filmmaker assumes the role of a co-creator, participating in Divine creativity.

The significance of narrative in Catholic tradition cannot be overstated. Jesus himself used parables, stories of everyday life, to reveal the mysteries of the Kingdom of God. In a parallel manner, cinema weaves narratives that can unveil the divine in the mundane, inviting viewers to a deeper reflection on their lives and the world around them. This narrative approach enables films to open spaces for spiritual insight and revelation.

Consider the sacramentality of film. Just as sacraments are outward signs that confer grace, films, too, can serve as vehicles of grace. They can touch hearts, provoke introspection, and even lead to moments of conversion. The visuality of cinema, with its capacity to show rather than tell, engages the viewer in an active process of seeing, not just with the eyes but with the soul.

This sacramental vision challenges filmmakers to approach cinema with a sense of reverence and responsibility. Crafting stories that resonate with truth and beauty demands a deep understanding of both craft and faith. It calls for attentiveness to the human experience, in all its complexity and sanctity, as a reflection of the divine.

Yet, representing Catholicism in film is fraught with challenges. The risk of reductionism, of trivializing the profound, is ever-present. Moreover, navigating the contemporary cultural landscape, where relativism often prevails, requires discernment and courage.

Filmmakers must strive to convey the Catholic vision in a way that is authentic, compelling, and accessible to a diverse audience.

The potential for evangelization through cinema is immense. In an age marked by visual culture, films have the power to reach individuals who might never enter a church or pick up a religious text. Cinema can sow seeds of faith, stirring curiosity and opening pathways to further exploration of the Gospel.

Films that intricately weave Catholic themes invite viewers into a dialogue—a dialogue not only with the creators and the characters but with themselves and God. This interactive nature of cinema, its ability to evoke questions and foster reflection, makes it a unique tool in the mission of the New Evangelization.

Moreover, the communal aspect of film viewing echoes the communal nature of the Church. Watching a film, whether in a theater or with a group at home, is an inherently communal experience. It gathers individuals together, not only to share in the act of viewing but to partake in the subsequent reflection and conversation. This communal dimension aligns with the Catholic understanding of faith as something lived and experienced in community.

Importantly, the Catholic tradition of storytelling, with its emphasis on beauty, truth, and goodness, can offer a counter-narrative to the prevailing trends of nihilism and despair in contemporary cinema.

Catholic filmmakers are tasked with the vocation of bearing witness to hope, to the reality of grace and redemption in a broken world. This does not mean shying away from the darkness but shining a light into it, portraying the victory of light over darkness, of life over death.

The diversity of Catholicism, with its various rites, traditions, and cultural expressions, also provides a rich palette for cinematic exploration. This diversity can help broaden the appeal of Catholic-themed films, making the universal messages of faith, love, and sacrifice accessible to a global audience.

As cinema continues to evolve, so too will its capacity to serve as a canvas for faith. Emerging technologies, new storytelling techniques, and the growing influence of digital platforms all present opportunities for creative engagement with the Gospel. The challenge for Catholic filmmakers is to harness these developments in a manner that remains true to the core of Catholic teaching while resonating with contemporary audiences.

In conclusion, the convergence of film, media, and Catholic storytelling holds great promise for the evangelization and formation of hearts and minds. Cinema, as a canvas for faith, offers a unique and powerful medium through which to convey the beauty, truth, and goodness of the Catholic tradition to a world in dire need of hope. As artists and faithful alike, we are called to support and participate in this creative mission, for the greater glory of God and the sanctification of the world.

The Challenges of Presenting Catholicism in Modern Media As we progress through the digital age, the depiction and incorporation of Catholicism in modern media face multifaceted challenges. The very essence of conveying a tradition that spans over two millennia into forms consumable by the fleeting attention spans of today's audience is an art form in itself. This section aims to unravel these challenges, seeking pathways that respect the depth of Catholic thought and art, while adapting to contemporary media landscapes.

The first challenge lies in the nature of media consumption itself. The rapid pace at which content is consumed and discarded in the digital realm often contradicts the Catholic invitation to contemplation and reflection. Media platforms favor content that can capture immediate attention, often at the expense of depth and nuance. This format poses a significant challenge for presenting Catholicism, which is rich in history, tradition, and theological complexity. Crafting content that is both engaging and faithful to its roots requires a delicate balance.

Moreover, the pluralistic nature of modern societies means that Catholic content often competes in a marketplace of ideas where it's not just about the message, but how it's delivered. This calls for a creative reimagining of Catholic themes, making them accessible and appealing to a broader audience without diluting their essence.

Another challenge is the portrayal of Catholicism in mainstream media, which can sometimes border on stereotypes or focus on controversies rather than the faith's spiritual and cultural richness. This skewed representation can influence public perception, demanding a proactive approach from Catholic content creators to offer narratives that are both authentic and positive.

Language also presents a significant barrier. The terminologies and concepts used within Catholicism can be complex, oftentimes derived from ancient texts and theological discourse. Translating these into the everyday language of modern media without losing their theological significance is a task that requires both wisdom and creativity.

The visual representation of Catholicism in media is another point of consideration. The faith's rich artistic legacy, from sacred art to liturgical vestments, needs to be presented in a way that resonates with today's visual culture while preserving its sacral integrity. Achieving this balance is crucial for engaging a society that is increasingly driven by visual communication.

Fostering engagement with younger generations, who are the primary consumers of digital media, offers another layer of complexity. This demographic often seeks authenticity and directness, values that can seem at odds with more traditional forms of religious expression. Finding a voice that resonates with younger audiences without compromising on the depth of Catholic teaching requires not just creativity but also a deep understanding of the concerns and questions that animate this generation.

Interactivity and participation, key components of digital media, offer both a challenge and an opportunity for presenting Catholicism. The interactive nature of social platforms can encourage a participatory form of engagement with faith. However, it also means navigating the risks associated with online discourse, including misinformation and divisiveness.

The global nature of modern media also means that Catholic content must be sensitive to cultural differences and open to inter-religious dialogue. This global perspective requires a nuanced understanding of how Catholicism intersects with diverse cultures and beliefs, making the universal message of the Gospel relevant to a multiplicity of contexts.

In addition, the challenge of monetization cannot be overlooked. Producing high-quality content that is both compelling and catechetical requires resources. Finding models for sustainable production that do not compromise the message for the sake of commercial success is a challenge facing many Catholic content creators.

The rise of independent content creators in the digital space opens up new avenues for presenting Catholicism. These creators can offer more personalized and nuanced reflections of faith. However, this also means ensuring that such content remains true to Catholic teaching amidst the decentralized and unregulated nature of digital platforms.

Concluding on a note of hope, despite the myriad challenges, the digital age offers unprecedented opportunities for evangelization and artistic expression. By embracing both the new and the ancient, Catholic content creators can navigate the modern media landscape with integrity and imagination, bringing the light of faith to the screens and hearts of a global audience.

Chapter 22: The Digital Continent: New Arenas for Evangelization

As the narrative unfolds from the tangible to the intangible, the Catholic imagination is called to venture into uncharted territories. Among these, the digital continent emerges as a profound space for evangelization, harmonizing the timeless essence of our faith with the incessant progress of technology. This chapter seeks to explore how the vibrancy of Catholic art can transcend traditional mediums, flourishing within the vast, interconnected realms of the digital age.

At the heart of this exploration lies the recognition that social media platforms and digital spaces are not mere tools or afterthoughts but fertile grounds for sowing the seeds of faith. Much like Paul the Apostle utilized the Roman roads and epistles to spread the Gospel, contemporary Catholic artists and evangelists are called to embrace digital venues as modern-day Areopags. Here, art becomes a beacon of hope and truth, illuminating the screens that dominate our daily lives with reflections of divine beauty.

The emergence of virtual art and spaces of worship further exemplifies the Church's journey into the digital continent. These virtual sanctuaries offer an oasis of spirituality amid the cacophony of the digital marketplace. Through livestreamed liturgies, online prayer groups, and digital recreations of sacred spaces, the Church extends her embrace, welcoming all to encounter the Divine, irrespective of physical boundaries.

However, navigating this new frontier demands a discerning heart and a creative spirit. The principles of sacramentality call for a profound integration of form and substance, ensuring that the content we share and create online truly reflects the transcendent beauty of God. As such, Catholic artists and creators are tasked with a sacred responsibility: to mold the digital clay with both reverence and innovation, crafting works that speak to the soul and awaken a thirst for the Divine.

Furthermore, the digital continent challenges us to rethink evangelization. Engagement in this realm transcends mere aesthetics; it involves creating a dialogue, fostering community, and offering a testimony of faith that resonates with the digital generation. It's about transforming the often fragmented and polarized spaces of social media into platforms for unity, understanding, and spiritual enrichment.

Yet, as we venture further into this digital landscape, we must also be wary of the dangers that lurk within. The addictive allure of virtual affirmation, the echo chambers of ideological conformity, and the loss of authentic human connection threaten to undermine the evangelical mission. The artistic calling within this digital continent, therefore, is not just to evangelize but to humanize, bridging pixels with the palpable, human warmth of Christ's love.

In this mission, the examples of contemporary Catholic artists and creators shine as beacons of hope. Through their innovative use of digital media, they reveal the enduring relevance of Catholic thought and culture. Their works serve not only as artifacts of faith but also as invitations to a deeper engagement with the mysteries of our existence, encouraging a dialogue that spans both heaven and earth.

As we look to the future, the digital continent holds untold potential for the evangelization and revitalization of Catholic culture. It beckons us to a new apostolate, one that embraces the vast possibilities of the digital age while remaining firmly rooted in the eternal truth of the Gospel. In this dynamic interplay of faith and technology, the Church finds a new canvas for her timeless mission: to illuminate the world with the beauty of Christ.

In conclusion, the venture into the digital continent is not merely an option but an imperative for the Catholic imagination. It is an affirmation that the Church, in her wisdom and creativity, can and must speak to the hearts of all, even across the digital expanse. As we continue to navigate these new arenas for evangelization, let us pray for the guidance of the Holy Spirit and the intercession of the saints, that our efforts may bear fruit in this digital age for the greater glory of God.

Social Media and the Catholic Presence

In an era where the digital realm has become the new Agora, the Catholic Church finds itself navigating the waves of the information age with a mission to evangelize — a mission that requires adaptation and a reinvigoration of its presence in social media. This chapter delves into how the Church is extending its centuries-old tradition of evangelization into the dynamic and ever-evolving landscape of social media, making the gospel accessible to the digital continent.

At the heart of the Church's engagement with social media is an understanding of its power to connect, inspire, and mobilize. Platforms such as Twitter, Facebook, and Instagram have become the new piazzas where the faithful and the curious alike gather, seeking answers, community, and a sense of belonging. Here, the Church has an unmatched opportunity to showcase the beauty of Catholic art, thought, and culture, engaging both mind and soul in a quest for transcendence and meaning.

The intersection of social media and Catholic presence is marked by a strategic cultivation of beauty and truth. Through captivating imagery, compelling narratives, and thoughtful reflections, the Church aims not only to educate but also to enchant, drawing individuals into the deeper mysteries of faith. The use of digital platforms allows for a profound democratization of sacred art, making it accessible to all, regardless of geographical or socio-economic barriers.

However, this digital engagement is not without its challenges. The ephemeral and often superficial nature of social media content demands a careful balance between attracting attention and inviting contemplation. Catholic content creators are tasked with crafting messages that resonate with a generation accustomed to the rapid consumption of information, all while preserving the depth and integrity of the faith.

Witness, then, is an essential component of the Catholic presence on social media. The Church's teachings and traditions are brought to life through the personal stories and experiences of individuals who embody the faith in their daily lives. By sharing their journeys, struggles, and transformations, they offer authentic testimonies that touch hearts and provoke curiosity, encouraging others to explore the riches of Catholicism.

The role of social media in evangelization also extends to catechesis and formation. Platforms such as YouTube and online forums have become virtual classrooms, where theology, philosophy, and the arts are unpacked and discussed. In this way, social media serves not only as a tool for outreach but also as a means for deepening the understanding and practice of the faith among the faithful.

Furthermore, social media facilitates a unique form of communal prayer and spiritual solidarity. Initiatives like live-streamed Masses, online prayer groups, and virtual retreats have opened new avenues for worship and spiritual growth, especially during times when physical gathering is not possible. These digital spaces become sanctuaries where the global Catholic community can unite in prayer, reflecting the universality and timelessness of the Church.

Engaging with social media, the Church embraces the call to be a beacon of light in the digital age, illuminating the path to Christ through the fusion of timeless truths and contemporary mediums. This venture is not merely an adaptation to modernity but a strategic and deliberate effort to fulfill the mandate of the Great Commission in the context of today's digital culture.

As the Church continues to navigate the complexities of social media, it does so with the conviction that these platforms are not merely tools for communication but sacred spaces for encounter. In the vastness of the digital continent, the Church finds fertile ground to sow the seeds of faith, hope, and love, embarking on a journey of evangelization that transcends boundaries, bridges divides, and brings the light of Christ to all corners of the earth.

In conclusion, the Catholic presence on social media is both a testament to the Church's enduring adaptability and a beacon of hope in a world yearning for meaning. Through strategic engagement with these platforms, the Church extends its mission of evangelization to the digital continent, inviting all to discover the beauty, truth, and goodness of the Catholic faith.

Virtual Art and Spaces of Worship In the continuum of Catholic creativity and evangelization, the digital age has ushered a novel canvas and sanctuary – the virtual domain. As pilgrims in a new Digital Continent, the Church's artistic and liturgical expressions find themselves migrating into realms that Dante or Michelangelo could scarcely have imagined. This progression is not merely an extension of physical reality but the birth of new landscapes for divine encounter.

The concept of virtual spaces of worship isn't merely about replicating the architectural grandeur of cathedrals or the sacred ambiance of a chapel within the digital world. It's about redefining the essence of sacred spaces, extending the reach of Catholic art and creating immersive experiences that evoke the transcendent in the hearts of the digital congregation. These virtual sanctuaries offer infinite possibilities for exploration, reflection, and prayer, transcending the limitations of time and geography.

Virtual art, in its essence, reflects the dynamic interplay between innovation and tradition. It's a domain where the timeless beauty and profound theological insights of Catholic art are infused with contemporary modes of digital expression. Through virtual reality (VR) experiences, faithful and seekers alike can venture through digital renditions of the Via Crucis, experience the Sistine Chapel ceiling with a heavenward gaze, or embark on virtual pilgrimages to the Holy Land.

This digital migration does not signify a departure from the physical expressions of faith but rather an expansion of the Church's mission to evangelize. As St. John Paul II eloquently articulated, the Church must be present in the 'Areopagus of modern times', engaging with the culture of the digital age to bring the Gospel's light to new frontiers (John Paul II, 1990).

The creation of virtual art and spaces of worship necessitates a unique fusion of talents – theologically informed artists, technologically adept architects, and visionary liturgists. These creators are tasked with an extraordinary mission: to transcend the binary code and pixels, ensuring that every virtual chapel and digital artwork serves as a conduit of grace, inviting an encounter with the Divine.

Virtual spaces dedicated to worship often incorporate interactive elements, such as clickable icons for prayer intentions or virtual candles that can be 'lit' as an offering. These elements, while symbolic, foster a sense of active participation among the faithful, mirroring the communal and participatory nature of Catholic worship.

The sacramental imagination of the Church finds a new expression in these virtual realms. While the sacraments themselves cannot be conferred digitally, virtual art and spaces can deeply enrich the catechetical preparation and spiritual formation of the faithful. They serve as a preparatory ground, kindling the desire for the tangible grace conferred through the physical sacraments.

Moreover, these digital expressions of faith are particularly significant in the context of the New Evangelization. They serve as a beacon for those who, for various reasons, might be marginalized or alienated from traditional forms of church community. The virtual spaces become a bridge, a welcoming hand extended into the digital expanse, inviting all to explore the richness of the Catholic faith.

One critical challenge facing these virtual expressions of Catholic art and worship is ensuring the authenticity of experience. Creators endeavor to craft experiences that are not only aesthetically engaging but are imbued with profound theological depth and liturgical accuracy. The aim is to create virtual environments that elevate the soul, remind of the sacred, and inspire a deeper yearning for God.

Another dimension to consider is the communal aspect of worship. The Church is fundamentally a community of believers, and this communal dimension must be ingenously integrated into virtual spaces. Through live-streamed Masses, prayer groups, and interactive forums, these digital sanctuaries strive to cultivate a sense of fellowship among participants, reflecting the universal communion of the Church.

As with any form of art, virtual art and spaces of worship offer a powerful medium for contemplation and transformation. They are invitations to step beyond the distractions of daily life and enter into a contemplative space, engaging with the mysteries of faith in a manner that resonates with the digital age's visual and interactive culture.

The ethical considerations inherent in the creation of virtual art and spaces are manifold. Creators navigate questions of accessibility, ensuring these spiritual resources do not perpetuate a digital divide but are available to all, irrespective of socio-economic realities. Accountability and integrity in representing the sacred traditions and teachings of the Church are paramount, maintaining a balance between innovation and reverence.

The evolution of virtual art and spaces dedicated to worship is a testament to the Church's enduring adaptability and commitment to evangelization. It's an acknowledgment that the call to encounter God isn't confined to stained glass and stone walls but extends into the digital vastness, meeting people where they are – in the midst of their digital lives.

In conclusion, the emergence of virtual art and spaces of worship represents a significant evolution in the way the Catholic Church engages with the faithful and the world at large. It's a journey of faith that traverses beyond the physical, reaching into the digital realm to touch the soul with beauty, invite into presence, and inspire a deepened relationship with the Divine.

Chapter 23: Contemporary Catholic Artists: Bearing Witness Today

In the tapestry of time, where each thread signifies an epoch, contemporary Catholic artists weave their narratives, embodying a testament to faith through the prism of modernity. At the heart of this endeavor lies the poignant mission to navigate the intricate challenges of the present age while steadfastly bearing witness to eternal truths. Thus, these artists undertake a sacred pilgrimage, armed with creativity and conviction, to echo the divine within the ephemeral landscapes of today.

The labyrinth of modern challenges that these artists face is multifaceted, spanning the realms of secular skepticism, digital transformation, and a rapidly shifting cultural ethos. In this context, the vocation of the Catholic artist transcends mere expression; it becomes an act of courageous testimony. Through their works, be it canvas, note, or verse, they assert the transcendental, affirming the presence of the divine amidst the temporal.

Their creative journey is marked by a profound engagement with the sacramental vision of reality. This vision, rooted in the incarnational essence of Catholic thought, propels them to discern and depict the holy in the mundane, the extraordinary in the ordinary. Thus, their art serves not only as a window to the divine but also as a mirror reflecting the viewer's search for meaning and transcendence.

Profiles of faith and creativity abound, where artists from diverse backgrounds and modalities share a common thread: the aspiration to incarnate the whispers of grace in their works. These narratives, rich in vulnerability and vigor, reveal the depths of their struggle to coalesce personal faith with artistic endeavor. Through their testimonies, one perceives a mosaic of modern saints, whose lives are consecrated not in chapels, but in studios, stages, and street corners.

The dialogue between faith and culture these artists engage in is not a monologue but an invitation. An invitation to explore the sacred within the secular, to question, to delve deeper, to confront the dissonance between creed and contemporary life. It is in this sacred space of questioning that faith is refined, and art becomes an instrument of revelation and conversion.

Notably, the medium through which these contemporary voices articulate their witness is as variegated as the spectrum of human experience. From the digital brushstrokes of virtual artistry to the tangible textures of sculpture, from the ineffable beauty of sacred music to the rhythmic cadences of poetry, each modality offers a unique locus for encounter with the divine.

Yet, the evolving landscape of art and technology presents both an opportunity and an ordeal. Social media, while a forum for unprecedented outreach, also harbors the peril of commodification, where the sacred risks being subjugated to the secular. Herein lies a critical challenge: to harness these new arenas without diluting the essence of the sacred art form, preserving its capacity to sanctify and inspire.

In response to these challenges, contemporary Catholic artists are called to a renewed fidelity to the Magisterium, anchoring their creative endeavors in the rich theological and philosophical heritage of the Church. This fidelity does not stifle creativity but rather deepens it, providing a firm foundation upon which imagination can soar in service of the transcendent.

Ultimately, the witness of contemporary Catholic artists is a beacon of hope, illuminating the path towards the divine amidst the shadows of doubt and disillusionment. Their art becomes a testament to the enduring power of beauty to convey truth, challenge perspectives, and transform hearts. In their hands, creativity is not a mere talent but a sacred calling, a means of sanctification for both the artist and the audience.

In conclusion, as we traverse the evolving landscape of contemporary Catholic art, we are reminded of the essential role of the artist as both prophet and pilgrim. Through their creative pilgrimage, they bear witness to the Light of the World, guiding humanity towards a renewed encounter with beauty, truth, and ultimately, the divine.

Navigating Modern Challenges

The spiritual and artistic journey of contemporary Catholic artists unfolds amidst a landscape proliferated with both profound opportunity and daunting challenges. These creators, vessels of divine inspiration, stand at the crossroads of tradition and innovation, navigating the complexities of a rapidly evolving world. Their artistry, deeply intertwined with their faith, endeavors not merely to create but to testify—to bear witness to the transformative power of beauty and truth in an era often marked by relativism and dissonance.

One of the significant trials faced by these artists is the dichotomy between the sacred and the secular in the public sphere. In a culture that increasingly marginalizes religious expressions and confines them to the private domain, Catholic artists strive to convey spiritual messages that resonate universally. Their work becomes a bridge, a dialogical encounter that invites onlookers into a contemplative space beyond the immediate, tangible world.

The digital age presents another double-edged sword. While technology offers unprecedented platforms for evangelization and artistic dissemination, it also engenders a milieu saturated with ephemeral content and fleeting attention spans. The challenge for Catholic artists is to harness these new mediums in a manner that captivates and conveys the eternal amidst the transitory. They must navigate the tension between leveraging digital tools for broader reach and maintaining the depth and solemnity of their sacred message.

Furthermore, the commodification of art poses a profound challenge. In a market-driven society, artistic value is often gauged by commercial success, a metric that can be at odds with the spiritual and catechetical imperatives of Catholic art. Artists committed to bearing witness through their creations are thus tasked with transcending the confines of commercial viability to pursue a higher calling—a vocation that prioritizes transformative impact over profit.

Moreover, the global nature of contemporary society, while enriching, also complicates the catholic (universal) appeal of this art. Creators must be cognizant of diverse cultural contexts, sensitivities, and expressions of faith, striving to craft works that are both particular and universal—embracing the Church's global nature while speaking to the local, individual experience of the divine.

The internal struggle for artistic authenticity also looms large. In an age where trends and hashtags often dictate creative directions, Catholic artists grapple with the challenge of staying true to their unique vision and voice. Their task is to forge artworks that are both relevant and resonant, engaging with contemporary dialogues while rooted in the timeless truths of their faith.

Despite these challenges, there lies a profound opportunity for contemporary Catholic artists to engage with the world in novel and meaningful ways. Their creations can become venues for encounter—spaces where the sacred and the secular meet, where the divine grace touches human experience. Through their work, artists have the potential to re-enchant the world, to unveil the luminous depth of reality hidden beneath the ordinary, beckoning society to look beyond itself towards the transcendent.

In navigating these modern challenges, the role of the Catholic artist transcends mere artistry; it assumes a prophetic dimension. These creators are called not just to bear witness to the beauty of creation but to participate in the salvific narrative, using their talents to draw others into a deeper understanding of their faith and ultimately, closer to the Divine.

In essence, the path of the contemporary Catholic artist is marked by a dual fidelity: to the integrity of one's art and to the truth of the Gospel. It is a journey fraught with obstacles but imbued with infinite potential—a pilgrimage towards the true, the good, and the beautiful, undertaken for the greater glory of God.

Moving forward from the profound discussions surrounding the modern challenges faced by Catholic artists, this section, **"Profiles in Faith and Creativity"**, delves into the lives and works of individuals who have brilliantly navigated the complexities of expressing their faith through art in contemporary times. These profiles serve as a testament to the notion that talent, when aligned with divine grace, becomes a powerful medium for education, conversion, and ultimately, salvation.

In exploring the lives of these artists, we discern a common thread: an unwavering commitment to their faith that remarkably influences their creative process. Their stories, marked by struggles and triumphs, offer invaluable insights into how art, in its myriad forms, can become a profound expression of the Catholic imagination in the 21st century.

One notable figure is a sculptor whose work has redefined the perception of sacred art in modern churches. His sculptures, characterized by a blend of traditional symbolism and contemporary design, encourage the beholder to experience the divine in a new dimension. The artist's approach to his craft is a profound reflection on the incarnation—God becoming flesh—and this theological insight becomes palpably present in his art. Through his sculptures, he invites viewers to encounter God not as a distant deity but as Emmanuel, God with us.

Another remarkable profile is that of a painter whose canvases are vibrant testimonies of the Catholic faith. Unlike the passive forms often seen in religious art, her figures are dynamic, full of movement and life, echoing the vivacity of the saints she depicts. She draws inspiration from the communion of saints, portraying them not just as historical figures, but as present companions in the journey of faith. Her work is a visual exegesis, a painted sermon, that calls the viewer to a deeper engagement with the mysteries of faith.

Music, with its ethereal quality, has been a traditional medium through which the transcendent has been experienced. In this context, the journey of a composer who integrates ancient Gregorian chants with contemporary musical elements illustrates the timeless relevance of Catholic tradition. His compositions are a dialogue between heaven and earth, where ancient melodies meet modern harmonies, inviting the listener into the eternal now of God's presence.

The digital continent, with its vast potential for evangelization, has seen the emergence of Catholic artists who leverage new media to proclaim the Gospel message. One such innovator has created a series of virtual reality experiences based on scenes from the Gospels. These immersive experiences allow individuals to encounter Christ in a way that is profoundly personal, breaking down barriers to faith for the modern viewer. His work exemplifies how technology, when harnessed for the glory of God, can become a frontier for new forms of artistry and evangelization.

Amidst the rise of secular ideologies, a writer courageously pens novels that explore themes of grace, redemption, and the human capacity for transcendence. Her narratives wrestle with the complexities of contemporary life, yet are imbued with a hope that is distinctly rooted in her Catholic faith. Through her storytelling, she articulates a vision of the world that is deeply sacramental, where ordinary elements of creation become conduits of divine grace.

These profiles, along with others, highlight the diverse ways in which Catholic artists today embody a faith that informs, inspires, and integrates their creative endeavors. Their lives and works attest to the vitality of the Catholic artistic tradition, proving that even in the face of modern challenges, art remains an eloquent language of faith.

Through their dedication, these artists demonstrate that creativity, infused with faith, possesses the capacity to not only beautify the world but to transform hearts. In this age of rapid change and uncertainty, their work becomes a beacon of hope, pointing towards the transcendent, reminding us of the eternal beauty that draws all creation towards its Creator.

Chapter 24: Towards a Theology of Beauty

The pursuit of beauty has, for millennia, been a compelling force in human experience, an allure that draws seekers towards the transcendent, towards that which is beyond the mere physical or material. The Catholic tradition, rich in its appreciation for the arts, suggests that beauty is not an end in itself but a path that leads to God. This chapter seeks to explore the intricate relationship between beauty and divinity, positing that the contemplation and creation of beauty can be a profound form of worship and a means of encounter with the Divine.

In the heart of Catholic theology lies the conviction that God is the source of all beauty. Creation itself is a testament to this truth, a grand canvas painted by the Divine Artist, inviting humanity to marvel, contemplate, and ultimately see beyond the creation to the Creator. The world, in its splendor and complexity, points towards a beauty that is eternal, not bound by time or space. It is here, amidst the wonders of creation, that one's journey towards understanding a theology of beauty begins.

Artistic expression within the Catholic tradition serves as a bridge between the earthly and the divine, between human experience and eternal truths. Artists, in their creative endeavors, partake in a divine act, echoing the Creator by bringing forth beauty that speaks of something greater than themselves. This understanding elevates art from mere decoration or entertainment to a sacred vocation, a means through which the invisible is made visible, and the divine is communicated to humanity.

The role of beauty and the arts in the Catholic tradition cannot be overstated. From the magnificence of Gothic cathedrals to the solemn beauty of Gregorian chant, the Catholic faith has historically understood and utilized beauty as a powerful means of drawing souls closer to God. This relationship between beauty and divinity is not solely for the enrichment of the individual soul but serves the communal aspect of worship, enhancing the liturgical experience and deepening the collective encounter with the sacred.

The sacramentality of beauty also plays a crucial role in Catholic thought. Just as the sacraments are outward signs of an inward grace, beauty too can be seen as a sign, a foretaste of the divine beauty that awaits in the Beatific Vision. This sacramental understanding of beauty suggests that experiences of beauty in this life are participations in the eternal beauty of God, and thus, every encounter with true beauty has the potential to be a moment of grace, an invitation to a deeper relationship with the Creator.

The Final Vocation of the Artist within the Catholic context is thus profoundly spiritual. Artists are called not only to create but to discern and reveal the presence of God in the world through their work. This vocational calling demands a cultivation of both skill and spirituality, a deepening of both craft and faith, so that through their art, artists might become mediators of the divine, helping others to see and appreciate the beauty that points towards God.

Understanding beauty as a path to God requires a disposition of openness, a willingness to be moved and transformed by encounters with beauty. It challenges the modern conception of art as subjective and beauty as merely in the eye of the beholder, proposing instead that true beauty, while it may evoke different responses, has an objective reality that participates in the beauty of God. This perspective opens up a rich dialogue between faith and reason, between theology and aesthetics.

In exploring the theology of beauty, it becomes evident that beauty, truth, and goodness are intimately connected. They are attributes of God that reflect in creation and through artistic expression. Catholic artists, in their pursuit of beauty, are also seekers of truth and proponents of goodness, contributing to the unveiling of the divine mystery in the world.

The implications of a theology of beauty extend beyond the realms of art and aesthetics into the moral and ethical dimensions of life. A deep appreciation for beauty fosters a culture of respect, reverence, and care for creation, countering the utilitarian and exploitative tendencies of contemporary society. By affirming the intrinsic value of beauty, the Catholic tradition calls for a stewardship of creation that recognizes and preserves its beauty as a testament to the Creator.

In conclusion, the journey towards a theology of beauty is both an invitation and a challenge. It invites us to see the world and our creative endeavors through the lens of faith, recognizing in them a reflection of divine beauty. It challenges us to transcend the superficial, to look beyond mere appearances, and to seek the eternal beauty that underlies all of creation. In doing so, we not only enrich our own lives but contribute to the sanctification of the world, making it a more fitting offering to the Creator of all that is beautiful.

Beauty as a Path to God

Within the sacred tapestry of Catholic tradition, beauty emerges as not merely an aesthetic attribute but as a divine conduit, a path that leads the soul towards God. This chapter delves into the profound idea that through beauty, both inherent in the natural world and manifested through human creativity, we can encounter the divine, transcend the mundane, and embark on a journey toward a deeper understanding and connection with our Creator.

The concept that beauty can serve as a bridge to the divine is deeply embedded in the fabric of Catholic thought. The Church, in her wisdom, has long recognized that beauty has the power to elevate the mind and heart, to pierce the veil of the ordinary, and to reveal glimpses of the extraordinary reality that lies beyond our immediate perception. It's through this encounter with beauty that we are invited to contemplate the ultimate Beauty, which is God Himself.

Sacred art and architecture provide a tangible manifestation of this path towards the divine. By stepping into a cathedral, one is enveloped in an atmosphere of transcendence. Every detail, from the soaring arches to the intricate stained glass windows, speaks a silent language of beauty that lifts the soul towards contemplation of the Divine Architect. Similarly, sacred music, with its harmonious layers and celestial qualities, has the capacity to transport the listener beyond the temporal realm, offering a foretaste of the heavenly liturgy.

But beauty as a path to God is not confined to the realms of art and architecture; it extends into the natural world, where the Creator's handiwork provides an ever-present reminder of His presence. The complexity of a single flower, the vast expanse of the night sky strewn with stars, the majestic mountains that pierce the heavens—all these are silent hymns of praise to the Creator, inviting the observer to a moment of awe, wonder, and ultimately, a deeper connection with the divine.

In engaging with beauty, whether through art, nature, or human interaction, we participate in an act of co-creation with the Divine. Our talents and creativity are gifts from God, meant to be nurtured and developed not for our glory, but for the greater purpose of leading ourselves and others closer to Him. This understanding of beauty and creativity as a cooperation with divine grace underscores the vocation of the artist in the Catholic tradition. The artist, through their work, becomes a mediator of the divine, translating the ineffable and the transcendent into forms that speak to the heart and lift the spirit.

However, the path of beauty towards God is not without its challenges. In a world often marred by brokenness and strife, beauty can seem elusive, obscured by the shadows of pain and suffering. Yet, it is precisely in these moments that the transformative power of beauty becomes most apparent. Beauty has the capacity to comfort, heal, and inspire hope; it reminds us of the presence of God even in the darkest times and calls us to a vision of the world as it was meant to be—a reflection of divine beauty and goodness.

Furthermore, the pursuit of beauty as a path to God requires discernment and intentionality. In a culture saturated with images and sounds that often distort the true nature of beauty, the Catholic artist must strive to create works that transcend mere aesthetic appeal, embodying instead the truth, goodness, and beauty that reflect the divine image. This pursuit is not solitary; it is supported and enriched by the community of faith, a communion of artists, thinkers, and believers who share the vision of beauty as a pathway to the Divine.

In conclusion, beauty, as understood within the Catholic imagination, offers a profound and luminous path towards God. It invites us to open our hearts and minds to the presence of the divine in the world around us, calling us to a journey of transformation. As we walk this path, let us embrace beauty in all its forms, allowing it to draw us ever closer to the source of all Beauty, to God Himself.

The Final Vocation of the Artist In the labyrinth of human endeavor, few quests are as mesmerizing and as fraught with celestial purpose as that of the Catholic artist. This vocation, one might argue, is the culminating point where heaven touches earth, where the divine spark within us seeks to illuminate the darkness of a world often blind to its own beauty. It's a journey that, while deeply personal, is never meant for the artist alone. Rather, it's a pilgrimage—a sacred journey undertaken for the sake of others, leading them closer to the transcendent, to the very heart of God.

The final vocation of the artist within the Catholic tradition is not just to create but to reveal. What does this entail? It means that every brushstroke, every note, every word penned with earnest intent, serves as a revelation of the divine. The artist, thus, becomes not just a creator but a conduit of divine grace, a mediator between the seen and the unseen, the temporal and the eternal (Vasari, 1550).

Art, in its most profound essence, serves as a window to the divine, encouraging the soul to gaze beyond the veil of the material world. The Catholic artist engages with creation, not as an end in itself, but as a means to glimpse the Creator. This sacred act of making visible the invisible is what distinguishes the artistic vocation as inherently salvific. Through their works, artists participate in God's continuing creation, echoing the divine Logos that spoke the cosmos into being.

The legacy of Catholic art as it unfolds through the annals of history—from the intricate mosaics of early Christian basilicas to the breathtaking Sistine Chapel ceiling—bears witness to this lofty

vocation. Each era, with its unique cultural expressions, has

contributed to the articulation of the faith in a language that

transcends words. This divine symphony of beauty serves not only

to instruct but also to elevate the soul, drawing it closer to the divine

mystery.

In the modern era, however, this vocation faces unprecedented

challenges. The secularization of society, the commodification of

art, and the pervasive skepticism towards transcendent truths have

obscured the path for many artists. Yet, it is precisely within this

context that the Catholic artist is called to witness. To bear light in a

world ensnared by shadows is no easy feat, yet it is both a duty and

an honor bestowed upon those who dare to see with the eyes of the

soul.

This final vocation entails a radical openness to the divine, a

willingness to be led where one might not choose to go. It requires

humility, for the artist must recognize that true beauty—beauty that

saves—is not of their making but a gift received and shared. This

receptivity transforms the artist's work into a form of prayer, a

ceaseless adoration of the One who is Beauty itself.

The Eucharist stands as the ultimate exemplar of this vocation. In

this holy sacrament, the mundane elements of bread and wine are

transubstantiated into the Body and Blood of Christ. Here, the

ultimate act of creation and redemption is made present, and the artist finds the source and summit of their calling. As participants in this divine mystery, Catholic artists are invited to let their creativity be similarly transubstantiated, becoming bearers of Christ to the world.

Thus emerges the artist's prophetic role, to echo God's whispers in a world deafened by noise. It is a call to remember what society has forgotten: that every human being is an image of the divine, that the world is charged with the grandeur of God. Through their creations, artists remind us of our origin and destiny, awakening a sense of wonder and a longing for the eternal.

Moreover, the final vocation of the artist is marked by hope. In a culture often characterized by despair, the creation of beauty is an act of defiance, a testament to the enduring presence of God despite the apparent triumph of darkness. This hope is not naive; it is grounded in the reality of the Resurrection, the ultimate victory of life over death, light over darkness.

Education and formation play crucial roles in nurturing this vocation. Just as the disciples on the road to Emmaus were unable to recognize Christ until the breaking of the bread, so too might we fail to perceive the divine presence in our midst without the proper formation. The Catholic artist must be steeped in the rich tradition of the Church, versed in the language of the saints and the mystics, for it is here that one finds the vocabulary of the Spirit.

In conclusion, the final vocation of the artist is nothing less than a call to sainthood. It is a journey that demands everything: talent, effort, and above all, love. For to create beauty—true beauty—is to participate in the act of love that birthed the universe. It is to affirm that, despite the shadows that beset us, the light of Christ shines undimmed, inviting us through beauty to return to our first and final Love.

In this sacred undertaking, the artist becomes a beacon of hope, a signpost pointing towards the divine, urging us onward on our journey home. And perhaps, in the end, this is the greatest art form of all: to live one's life as a masterpiece, crafted under the gentle yet relentless hand of the divine Artist, until we are finally transfigured into the image we were always meant to reflect.

Chapter 25: The Artist as Prophet and Pilgrim

In the sacred journey of Catholic artistry, the artist embodies a dual role, acting both as a prophet to society and a pilgrim navigating the terrain of personal sanctification. This chapter explores the profound calling of Catholic artists to serve not merely as creators of aesthetic objects but as visionaries and sojourners, whose creative endeavors are intrinsically linked to their quest for the Divine.

At the heart of the Catholic artist's vocation is the prophetic mission. Like the prophets of old, who bore God's message to His people, artists are tasked with unveiling the divine mysteries hidden within the fabric of creation. Through their work, they articulate the ineffable, translate the intangible, and give form to the transcendent, thereby participating in God's ongoing revelation. In this light, the artist's studio becomes akin to the prophet's wilderness, a place of solitary communion and confrontation with the divine mystery.

However, the call of the Catholic artist extends beyond the mere communication of divine truths. It involves a pilgrimage—a continual journey of transformation both inward and toward the ultimate source of all beauty, God Himself. This pilgrimage is not a linear progression but a spiral ascent, where the artist encounters God's grace anew at each turn, allowing for deeper integration of faith and creative practice.

Living as both prophet and pilgrim requires a profound spiritual grounding. The artist must cultivate a life of prayer and sacrament, engaging deeply with the Church's liturgical and sacramental life. In the rhythm of the liturgical year and the grace of the sacraments, the artist finds the wellspring of inspiration and the strength necessary for their vocation.

The dual identity of the artist as prophet and pilgrim also places them within a community of fellow seekers—both within the Church and in the wider society. Their work thus becomes a bridge, inviting others into a journey toward the true, the good, and the beautiful. By weaving their personal encounter with the Divine into the fabric of human experience, they beckon others closer to the heart of the Church.

However, this path is not without its challenges. The modern world often regards faith with skepticism, if not outright hostility. The Catholic artist, therefore, must possess courage—the courage to stand as a sign of contradiction, to create what the world may not yet understand, and to hold fast to the truth in a sea of relativism.

Ultimately, the vocation of the Catholic artist is a witness to hope. In a culture often marred by despair and cynicism, the artist affirms the possibility of redemption, the reality of beauty, and the presence of God in the midst of human life. Their work proclaims that, beyond the shadows of this world, the light of the Divine shines undiminished.

In conclusion, the Catholic artist's journey as prophet and pilgrim is a profound testament to the power of beauty to draw hearts toward the ultimate Beauty, who is God. Through their creative endeavors, artists participate in the divine creativity, pointing the way to the source of all beauty and truth. Thus, they fulfill their sacred calling, contributing to the sanctification of the world and the salvation of souls.

The Role of the Artist in the Church

In the grand tapestry of Christian tradition, artists carve out a sacred space, weaving threads of the divine into the fabric of human experience. Their role, richly multifaceted, extends far beyond the creation of aesthetically pleasing objects. Instead, artists within the Church embody the dual mantle of prophet and pilgrim, tasked with a divine vocation that bridges heaven and earth, whispering truths of the transcendent into the ear of the temporal.

At its heart, the Church recognizes the artist as a vessel through which the Holy Spirit can articulate the ineffable truths of faith, hope, and love. This recognition is not merely an acknowledgment of the artists' talent as a personal gift but as a divine instrument intended for the common good (Catechism of the Catholic Church, 1994). By drawing from the wellspring of divine creativity, artists become co-creators with God, shaping matter and spirit in ways that reveal the sacred in the midst of the profane.

Historically, the Church has championed the arts as a medium of revelation. From the majesty of Michelangelo's Sistine Chapel to the humility of a parish fresco, art has served as a conduit for spiritual enlightenment and catechesis. It educates not only the intellect but also the heart, inviting an encounter with the divine that is as personal as it is communal. Through beauty, artists herald a glimpse of the eternal kingdom, crafting echoes of Eden that stir the soul towards contemplation and prayer.

The prophetic role of the artist emerges in their ability to see beyond the veil of the ordinary, to discern the brushstrokes of God in the mundane. By presenting the world transfigured by the light of Christ, artists challenge society's narratives, confronting the darkness of the age with the hope of the Gospel. This prophetic witness hinges not on the didactic or explicit but on the capacity of beauty to pierce the heart, inviting conversion in subtle whispers rather than thunderous decrees.

As pilgrims, artists tread the sacred path of human longing and divine pursuit. Their journey reflects the broader pilgrimage of the Church towards its eschatological fulfillment. Embracing a vocation of beauty, artists navigate through the tension of the already and the not yet, crafting works that reflect their personal quest for truth while guiding others towards the heavenly homeland. This pilgrim aspect recognizes the unfinished masterpiece of creation, with artists participating in the ongoing work of redemption.

Moreover, the liturgical life of the Church offers artists a unique canvas for their spiritual imagination. In the rhythms of the liturgical calendar, artists find the narrative arc of salvation history—an endless source of inspiration. Sacred art and music, crafted for liturgical purposes, not only enriches the worship experience but also deepens the communal encounter with the mysteries of faith. Through these works, the artist helps to scaffold the bridge between the transcendent God and the immanent worship community.

In a world increasingly disenchanted with the material, the artist calls attention to the sacramentality of existence. Each brushstroke, note, or word becomes a testament to the incarnational reality that underpins Catholic imagination. This sacramental vision charges the natural world with a deeper significance, inviting a re-enchantment of creation that sees in it the fingerprints of the Creator.

Yet, the vocation of the Catholic artist is not without its trials. The challenge to remain true to the Gospel while navigating the demands and critiques of both the Church and the secular world can be daunting. Moreover, the pursuit of authentic beauty—a beauty that transcends mere aesthetics to touch upon the truth—is a narrow path laden with the risk of misunderstanding and rejection. Nevertheless, it is precisely in embracing these challenges that the artist's work becomes a true act of faith, a testament to the power of grace working through human creativity.

In conclusion, the artist in the Church stands as a beacon of hope, a sign of contradiction to a culture of immediacy and disposability. Through their dedication to beauty, artists affirm the inherent dignity and value of creation, inviting all to look beyond the horizon of the temporal towards the eternal. In this sacred calling, artists not only depict the glories of the celestial kingdom but also illuminate the path towards it, guiding the faithful as both prophets and pilgrims in the world.

Living the Vocation of Beauty

In the kaleidoscopic expanse of Catholic tradition, the vocation of beauty emerges as a sacred path, inviting artists to transcend the temporal and touch the divine. This vocation is not merely an avocation or hobby but a profound calling that aligns the creative spirit with the eternal dialogue between creation and Creator. It's a vocation marked by the relentless pursuit of truth, goodness, and beauty, all reflections of God's essence. Engaging with this calling requires understanding its depth, embracing its challenges, and embodying its principles in the artistry of everyday life.

At the heart of living this vocation is the recognition of beauty as a divine attribute, a tangible sign of God's presence among us. Through beauty, the invisible is made visible, the untouchable is felt, and the inaudible is heard. Catholic teaching has long promulgated that beauty does more than delight the senses—it acts as a beacon guiding the soul towards divine mystery. This understanding elevates the artist's role from mere craftsman to co-creator with God, tasked with revealing truths about the human experience and the divine through their work.

The artist, in their studio or workspace, becomes akin to an altar, a sacred space where heaven and earth meet. Each brushstroke, note, or word is an invocation, a prayer that materializes on canvas, in melody, or on paper, inviting participation in the divine. This sacred act is not confined to the traditionally 'holy' or expressly religious but encompasses all creation that seeks the upliftment of the human spirit towards the good and the beautiful, reflecting the ultimate Creator.

To live the vocation of beauty means to see the world through the lens of sacramentality, where ordinary elements carry extraordinary grace. Just as sacraments in the Catholic Church signify and impart grace, so too does art become a conduit of divine meaning, transforming the mundane into the sacred. The artist, therefore, is tasked with a profound responsibility: to hone their skill and craft in service of this higher purpose, to be diligent stewards of the talent entrusted to them by God.

Living this vocation also demands a commitment to authenticity and integrity, for the pursuit of beauty is not only about aesthetic pleasure but about the expression of truth. It requires vulnerability and courage, as true art often demands the sharing of one's innermost self, the depths of one's soul, and the contemplation of life's great mysteries. This act of sharing becomes a form of evangelization, where the artist's work can speak to hearts in ways words cannot, opening doors to the divine for themselves and others.

Moreover, this vocation is a journey, not a destination. It is a path that asks for continual learning, growth, and openness to the Spirit's movements. Artists are called to be pilgrims, constantly seeking, exploring, and allowing the beauty they create and encounter to transform them. This pilgrimage is one of both inward reflection and outward expression, influencing not only the artist's work but their very being.

Community plays an integral role in living the vocation of beauty. The artist, while often working in solitude, is part of a greater communion of creators, past and present, who share this divine calling. There is a fellowship in this shared journey, a mutual understanding and support that connects artists across time and space. This community offers encouragement, inspiration, and challenge, pushing each member towards greater depth in their work and faith.

In practical terms, living this vocation might manifest in various forms, from the creation of art that explicitly explores religious themes to art that, while perhaps secular in content, is imbued with a sense of the sacred and seeks to elevate the viewer's mind and heart. It can also involve the cultivation of beauty in everyday life, recognizing and nurturing the inherent artistry in the mundane, thus sanctifying it.

The vocation of beauty is not without its challenges. The modern world often places utility and profit above beauty, and the artist may struggle to find their place within it. Yet, it is precisely in this context that the call to create beauty becomes ever more urgent, as a counter-sign to the commodification of culture and the desacralization of the world. The challenge, then, becomes an opportunity—to witness to the transformative power of beauty, to heal and elevate the culture through the infusion of the sacred into the secular.

Discernment is crucial for the artist navigating the tension between artistic freedom and faithfulness to the Church's teachings. This discernment involves constant prayer, dialogue with the community, and an honest evaluation of one's work and intentions. It's about ensuring that one's art serves the true, the good, and the beautiful and contributes to the sanctification of the world and the salvation of souls.

The Church, recognizing the indispensable value of art, offers both challenge and support to artists. Through her teachings, liturgy, and patronage, the Church has cultivated and safeguarded the sacredness of beauty throughout history. She understands that beauty has the power to open hearts to encounter God, and thus she calls upon artists to imbue their works with spirit and truth.

In conclusion, living the vocation of beauty is a profound, multifaceted calling that integrates faith, art, and life. It is a journey marked by continuous conversion to the beauty of God, a pilgrimage that seeks to manifest the divine through the tangible. For the artist called to this vocation, their work becomes a prayer, their creativity an act of worship, and their life a testament to the beauty of God's creation. It is, ultimately, a path towards sanctity, where the artist, through their devotion to beauty, participates in the redemption of the world.

For the Greater Glory of God

In traversing the vast landscapes painted by the Catholic imagination, one reaches a luminous vista at the journey's end—a place where all art converges in its noblest aim: ad maiorem Dei gloriam, for the greater glory of God. This tenet, the resounding echo throughout the corridors of Catholic thought, culture, and creativity, serves as both origin and destination for every genuine artistic endeavor under the heavens.

The exploration into the essence of Catholic creativity reveals a rich tapestry where the divine intertwines with the human, a sacred narrative woven through history from the catacombs to the splendor of the Renaissance. At its core, Catholic art acts as a sacramental sign, a window to the divine, offering glimpses of the eternal and invoking the divine presence in our everyday lives. Within this theological framework, talent emerges not merely as an individual gift but a divine entrustment, calling for stewardship in the service of the Almighty and the common good.

Viewing time as the canvas of divine artistry reminds us that our lives are part of a greater masterpiece. Liturgical time, with its rhythm and seasons, frames our creativity, inviting us into a deeper participation in the redemptive work of Christ through every brush stroke, note, and word penned. In the symphony of Catholic art, every form, be it sculpture, painting, or music, sings in harmony of a transcendent reality, guiding souls to contemplation and encounter with the divine.

Through the power of narrative, Catholic literature serves as a vessel for evangelization, educating and converting hearts across generations. Saints' lives inspire, philosophers and theologians offer cathedrals of thought, and scientists bridge the perceived chasm between faith and reason, all contributing to a chorus that celebrates the Creator of all.

The moral imagination of the Catholic artist faces modern challenges head-on, wrestling with presenting timeless truths through contemporary mediums. In political and social realms, art becomes a herald of justice and peace, shaped and informed by the Church's social teachings. Thus, Catholic art does more than beautify; it educates, reforms, and calls to action.

As the digital age unfolds, new frontiers for evangelization emerge. Social media and virtual spaces become canvases for faith, challenging the artist and the faithful to navigate these digital continents with ingenuity and purpose. Contemporary Catholic artists, living witnesses to faith in an often indifferent or hostile world, bear the torch passed through ages, illuminating the path for the seekers of truth.

The call to a theology of beauty, wherein beauty becomes a path to God, speaks to the final vocation of the artist. It is here, in the pursuit of the transcendental—truth, goodness, and beauty—that the artist mirrors the Creator, participating in the divine act of creation. This participation is not passive but prophetic, as the artist, in the role of prophet and pilgrim, discerns and declares the signs of the times.

To exist for the greater glory of God infuses every act of creation with profound purpose and meaning. This spiritual and cultural journey culminates not in the work itself but in the orientation of one's whole life and creative output toward the glorification of the divine. Such an endeavor requires both courage and humility, as the artist becomes a vessel through which the light of Christ is made manifest in the world.

In this light, the symbiosis between faith, culture, and art is not arbitrary but essential, a means by which the Church fulfills her mission to evangelize. Art, in its most elevated form, becomes a bridge between the human and the divine, a means of grace that draws the viewer, listener, or reader into a deeper communion with God.

This grand narrative, spanning centuries and traversing cultures, converges on a singular truth: beauty will save the world. In a society often marred by ugliness and discord, the Catholic artist is called to be a beacon of hope, crafting windows to heaven that invite all to look upward and beyond, to taste and see the goodness of the Lord.

As we stand on the threshold of the future, looking back at the legacy of Catholic creativity, let us move forward with a renewed zeal for the arts, dedicated to the propagation of the faith. Let the works created for the greater glory of God be our legacy, a testament to the enduring power of beauty to speak to the heart of humanity. In doing so, may we, together with the communion of saints and all creators of beauty, echo the sentiment of St. Ignatius of Loyola, dedicating our talents, our creativity, and our very selves to the greater glory of God.

In concluding, let us remember that our artistic endeavors are not just personal expressions but acts of worship and vehicles of grace. They fulfill a deeply communal and ecclesial function, linking the individual soul to the universal Church and, ultimately, to the divine. Through the sacred act of creation, artists partake in the divine creativity, becoming co-creators in the unfolding narrative of salvation history.

The journey of Catholic art is far from over. As we venture into unknown territories, may our creativity be guided by the Holy Spirit, fostering innovation while rooted in tradition. Let us envision a future where the Church and her artists continue to illuminate the dark corners of our world with the light of faith, hope, and beauty— always for the greater glory of God.

Thus, the canvas of the future is wide, the palette rich with divine promise. Armed with faith, hope, and love, let us, the artists and heirs of this great tradition, press on, painting, sculpting, writing, and singing for the greater glory of God. May our works, imbued with the spirit of the Gospel, serve as beacons of light in a world yearning for beauty and truth.

Appendix A: Appendix

Within the realm of Catholic thought, art isn't a mere adjunct to worship or pedagogy but a profound means of encountering the Divine. In pursuing this encounter, artists enter into a unique synergy with God's creative act, aligning their talents with divine intentions for the world's sanctification and enlightenment. This appendix aims to serve as a guiding beacon for those inspired by this holy pursuit.

A Gallery of Saints for Artists

The Gallery of Saints for Artists finds its root in the rich soil of Catholic tradition, where saints serve not only as intercessors but also as paragons of divine creativity manifesting through human cooperation with grace. Among these sanctified artists, Saint Luke, often honored as the patron saint of painters, emerges as a significant figure, attributed with painting the Virgin Mary. Saint Catherine of Bologna, a patroness of artists, offers inspiration through her devotion to art as a form of prayer and meditation. Saint John of the Cross, with his mystical poetry, exemplifies the depth of theological insight achievable through the marriage of faith and creativity. This gallery aims to remind Catholic artists that their endeavors are not solitary; they are part of a great communion of saints.

Resources for Further Exploration: Books, Films, Music, and Websites

This section comprises a curated compilation designed to foster a deeper understanding and appreciation of Catholic art's manifold dimensions. Among recommended books, "The Spirit of the Liturgy" by Joseph Cardinal Ratzinger (Pope Benedict XVI, 2000) elucidates the profound connections between liturgy, art, and aesthetics. For those drawn to visual narratives, the film "Of Gods and Men" (2010) offers a poignant exploration of faith, artistry, and sacrifice, telling the true story of Trappist monks in Algeria. In the realm of music, Hildegard of Bingen's compositions become a gateway to the ethereal interplay of sanctity and sound, weaving together theology and melody into a tapestry of celestial worship. Additionally, websites such as ArtWay (http://www.artway.eu) present an online portal to the world of sacred art, offering access to contemporary and historical works, essays, and reflections that bridge the gap between faith and artistic expression.

By delving into these resources, artists are invited to expand their horizons, absorbing insights that not only enhance their creativity but also anchor their work in a deeper sense of purpose and connection to the divine.

A Gallery of Saints for Artists

In the vast expanse of history, where divine grace intersects with human creativity, a multitude of saints stand as luminaries, guiding artists towards the sublime integration of faith and art. This gallery, not confined by any walls, spans across time and space, offering inspiration and patronage to those who seek to glorify God through their artistic endeavors. Here, we explore a selection of these celestial patrons, whose lives and legacies provide a fountain of inspiration for artists in their spiritual and creative journeys.

First among the pantheon of artistic guardians is Saint Luke the Evangelist. Traditionally heralded as the patron saint of painters, he is venerated for allegedly rendering the first icon of the Virgin Mary. His narrative evokes the profound connection between visual representation and the divine, urging artists to see their work as a form of evangelization, a sacred act of bearing witness to the ineffable mysteries of faith.

Saint Cecilia, revered as the patroness of musicians, embodies the ethereal link between music and the divine. Her steadfast faith, amidst the trials of martyrdom, whispers through the ages that music carries the power to elevate souls towards a higher contemplation of God. Artists in the musical domain look to her for inspiration, seeking to compose and perform works that resonate with the harmonies of heaven.

Turning to the realm of architecture, Saint Barbara stands tall. Her story, though shrouded in legend, speaks to the enduring strength of faith. With her patronage, architects are reminded that structures crafted by human hands can transcend their material existence, becoming sacred spaces that draw the faithful closer to the Divine Architect.

In the intricate dance of language and narrative, Saint John the Evangelist emerges as a guide for writers. His eloquent Gospel and Revelations, rich with symbolic imagery, serve as a testament to the power of the word. Authors, poets, and scholars look to him for the courage to wield their pens as swords of truth, carving out paths of enlightenment in the wilderness of the world.

The luminous path of painters is further illuminated by Saint Catherine of Bologna, patroness of artists. Her own artistic endeavors, coupled with deep spiritual insights, reveal the potential of visual arts to serve as a conduit of divine grace. She teaches that true beauty in art emanates from a soul intimately united with God.

For sculptors, Saint Claude de la Colombière offers a source of spiritual camaraderie. Though not an artist himself, his profound reflections on the Sacred Heart of Jesus inspire sculptors to imbue their works with the depth of divine love, shaping matter to reflect the contours of the sacred.

In the world of theater, Saint Genesius of Rome plays a central role. As a martyr who found faith on the stage, he exemplifies the transformative power of performance. Actors and playwrights invoke his name, seeking to infuse their works with the authenticity and courage that marked his conversion and martyrdom.

The cinematic arts find an exemplar in Saint Clare of Assisi, who, though living in a time far removed from the advent of film, is celebrated for her visionary spirituality. Filmmakers and those involved in media look to her life as a beacon, aspiring to create works that reflect the light of Christ in the digital age.

Saint Gabriel the Archangel, patron of telecommunications, serves as a celestial patron for those navigating the complexities of modern communication mediums. His role in delivering divine messages imparts lessons on clarity, integrity, and the power of words to bridge the divine and the human.

In the realm of photography, Blessed Fra Angelico is venerated for his transcendent frescoes. While not a photographer, his mastery in capturing divine light serves as an inspiration for photographers to pursue the luminous truth, striving to encapsulate moments of grace in their frames.

Dance, as an expression of the soul's movement towards God, finds a patroness in Saint Vitus, whose jubilant faith was manifested in physical exuberance. Dancers and choreographers seek his intercession, hoping their art may become a prayer, a bodily hymn of praise to the Creator.

Saint Elizabeth of Hungary, though not an artist in the conventional sense, exemplifies the artistry of charity. Her compassionate actions remind artists that their creations should not only seek aesthetic beauty but should also serve as vessels of love and compassion, touching hearts and healing wounds.

The tapestry of Catholic artists is further enriched by the witness of Blessed John of Fiesole, known as Fra Angelico. His life, dedicated to the creation of sacred art, stands as a testament to the unity of artistic talent and spiritual fervor. Artists of all kinds look to him as a model of integrating vocational calling with divine inspiration.

The legacy of Saint Gregory the Great, patron of musicians and singers, underscores the sacramental quality of music. His contributions to the liturgical tradition remind us that music is not merely an art form but a medium through which the divine whispers to the human heart.

This gallery, though incomplete, offers a glimpse into the communion of saints—each a unique hue in the spectrum of divine artistry. As artists draw inspiration from their stories, they embark on a journey not just of creating but of becoming themselves masterpieces of grace, reflecting the glory of the Creator through the canvas of their lives.

Resources for Further Exploration: Books, Films, Music, and Websites

In the pursuit of understanding the confluence of Catholic art, thought, and culture, one might find themselves longing for resources that can serve as both inspiration and education. The journey through Catholic creativity is vast and enriched not only by religious doctrine but also by the profound expressions of human experience through art. This section aims to curate a selection of books, films, music, and websites that encapsulate the essence of Catholicism's impact on art and culture. Each recommended resource is a testament to the eternal dialogue between the divine and the creative human spirit.

Books have long been the gatekeepers of knowledge, and in the realm of Catholic art, they serve as bridges between the past and present. *The Spirit of Catholicism* by Karl Adam offers an eloquent exploration of Catholic faith's core principles and their relevance today. Through its pages, one discovers the bedrock of Catholic thought that underpins the church's artistic expression. Another invaluable resource is *Sacred Pathways* by Gary Thomas, which delves into the unique ways individuals experience their relationship with God, inviting readers to see the act of creation as a form of worship.

Films have the power to manifest the unseen and speak to hearts in a universal language. *Of Gods and Men*, directed by Xavier Beauvois, portrays the lives of French Trappist monks living in Algeria, offering a poignant look at faith, sacrifice, and community. This film beautifully showcases the intersection of Catholic values with the challenges of the modern world. Meanwhile, *The Mission*, directed by Roland Joffé, uses the medium of cinema to tell a historically rich tale of Jesuit missionaries in South America, emphasizing themes of conversion, penance, and salvation that are central to Catholic teaching.

Music, with its ethereal quality, can touch the depths of the soul inaccessible to other forms of art. *Gregorian Chant* performed by the Benedictine Monks of Santo Domingo de Silos brings the ancient tradition of liturgical music into the homes and hearts of the listener, creating an environment conducive to meditation and prayer. Additionally, John Rutter's *Requiem* provides a contemporary interpretation of traditional Catholic liturgical music, blending elements of the old and new, sacred and secular.

The internet has become a vast repository of information where seekers of beauty and truth can find rich resources. *Vatican.va*, the official website of the Vatican, provides access to encyclicals, statements from the Pope, and archive material significant to the Catholic faith and its history. Another noteworthy website, *Sacred Space*, offers users daily guided meditations and prayers, grounding their exploration of art and faith in the Catholic tradition of contemplative prayer.

As explorers on this journey, it is essential to frequently return to the wellspring of primary texts that are the cornerstone of Catholic thought and art. The *Catechism of the Catholic Church* serves not only as a compendium of teachings but also as a mirror reflecting the integration of faith and reason, ritual, and imagery which are pivotal in understanding the Catholic contribution to the arts.

This curated collection, though far from exhaustive, provides a starting point for those eager to dive deeper into the ocean of Catholic art and culture. Each book, film, or piece of music, and every website recommendation is a thread in the vast tapestry of Catholic creative expression. They stand as beacons guiding the inquisitive mind and the yearning heart towards a richer understanding and appreciation of how the divine permeates all facets of human creativity. As such, these resources are more than just tools for learning -- they are invitations to experience the beauty and depth of Catholic tradition and inspire one's own creative explorations in faith.

In framing our exploration, let us remember that the act of creating, be it through words, images, or sounds, is a reflection of the Creator Himself. Through engaging with these resources, we partake in a tradition that not only preserves the past but also envisions the future. Let the study of Catholic art and culture be not just an academic endeavor but a transformative experience that echoes the sentiment 'ad majorem Dei gloriam' - for the greater glory of God.

Chapter 26: Acknowledgments

In the endeavor to explore the vast ocean of Catholic art and its impact on culture, thought, and spirituality, this journey would not have reached its destination without the collaboration and support of many. Indeed, this work, aiming to elucidate the eternal import of Catholic art, has been a cooperative venture with grace, mirrored in the talents and efforts of numerous individuals and communities.

Foremost, gratitude extends to the scholarly mentors who have guided this exploration with their profound knowledge and unwavering support. Their dedication to unraveling the mysteries of faith through the lens of art has been nothing short of inspirational. Among them, a special acknowledgment is due to those who have journeyed through the labyrinth of history, theology, and aesthetics, illuminating the path with their insights.

The academic institutions that have provided the resources and environment conducive to this study deserve special mention. Their libraries, replete with volumes of ancient wisdom and modern critique, were indispensable in this scholarly pursuit. Moreover, the vibrant discussions and debates within their halls have enriched this work immeasurably, enabling a deeper understanding of the Catholic artistic tradition.

Artists and creators, past and present, who have consecrated their talents to the divine, are the bedrock upon which this study stands.

Their masterpieces, serving as windows to the transcendent, have been a source of inspiration and awe throughout this endeavor. In exploring their works, one finds a tangible expression of the divine cooperation between human creativity and grace.

The communities of faith that have preserved and cherished these works of art over centuries deserve heartfelt thanks. Their devotion has ensured that the beauty and truth encapsulated in these artistic creations continue to enlighten and inspire souls across generations.

To the multitude of saints, whose lives and legacies have been examined in this work, a profound sense of gratitude is owed. Their embodiment of beauty through sanctity has provided a living commentary on the vocation of the artist in the service of truth and grace.

The patrons and benefactors who have supported this project, recognizing the value of articulating the relationship between Catholic thought and art, have been essential to its fruition. Their generosity and vision have facilitated a deeper exploration into the ways art serves as a means of salvation, education, and conversion.

Colleagues in the field of art history, theology, and philosophy have contributed significantly through their critiques, suggestions, and encouragement. Their scholarly camaraderie has been a source of strength and motivation, fostering a collaborative spirit that has greatly enriched this work.

The friends and family who have journeyed alongside, bearing witness to the countless hours of research and writing, have provided invaluable support. Their patience, understanding, and encouragement have been the underpinning of this endeavor, reminding of the broader community's role in the individual pursuit of knowledge and beauty.

Finally, recognition is due to the reader, whose interest in the intersection of Catholic art, thought, and culture has made this exploration not just a scholarly pursuit but a shared journey. It is hoped that this work serves as an invitation to delve deeper into the profound dialogue between faith and art, discovering therein a source of beauty, inspiration, and conversion.

In sum, this work stands as a testament to the communal effort in exploring the divine through art. It is a collaboration that spans not only contemporaries but reaches back through the ages, linking with those who have, through their own creativity and insight, sought to express the ineffable beauty of the divine. As such, this acknowledgment is not merely a closing gesture but an affirmation of the ongoing conversation between heaven and earth, mediated through the talents and vision of countless individuals who have contributed to the Catholic artistic tradition.

In this spirit, the conclusion of this work is not an end but an invitation to continue the exploration, inspired by the richness of tradition and the endless possibilities for future creativity. May the journey continue to inspire, educate, and transform, drawing ever closer to the Author of all beauty.

References

1. Gardner, H. (2016). Gardner's Art through the Ages: A Global History. Cengage Learning.

2. Norberg-Schulz, C. (1979). Genius Loci: Towards a Phenomenology of Architecture. Rizzoli.

3. John Paul II. (1999). Letter to Artists. Vatican City: Libreria Editrice Vaticana.

4. Vatican Council II. (1964). Inter mirifica, §11. Vatican City: Vatican website.

5. Caldecott, S. (2009). Beauty for Truth's Sake: On the Re-enchantment of Education. Brazos Press.

6. Pieper, J. (1998). Leisure, The Basis of Culture. Ignatius Press.

7. Aquinas, T. (1274). Summa Theologica.

8. Backhouse, J. (1981). The Lindisfarne Gospels. Phaidon.

9. Beauvois, X. (Director). (2010). Of Gods and Men [Film]. Why Not Productions.

10. Benedictine Monks of Santo Domingo de Silos. (1994). Gregorian Chant [Album]. Angel/EMI.

11. Catechism of the Catholic Church. (1993). 2nd ed. Vatican City: Libreria Editrice Vaticana.

12. Catechism of the Catholic Church. (1993). Libreria Editrice Vaticana.

13. Catechism of the Catholic Church. (1994). 2nd ed. Vatican: Libreria Editrice Vaticana.

14. Catholic Church. (1992). Catechism of the Catholic Church. Vatican City: Libreria Editrice Vaticana.

15. Catholic Church. (2020). Directory for Catechesis. Libreria Editrice Vaticana.

16. Conant, K. J. (1973). Carolingian and Romanesque Architecture: 800 to 1200. Penguin Books.

17. Dante Alighieri. The Divine Comedy. Translated by Henry Wadsworth Longfellow, Barnes & Noble Classics, 2005.

18. Dillenberger, J. (1999). The Religious Art of Pablo Picasso. University of California Press.

19. Dillenberger, J. (1999). The Visual arts and Christianity in America: From the colonial period to the present. Wipf and Stock Publishers.

20. Dreves, G. M., & Blume, C. (Eds.). (1901). Ein Jahrtausend lateinischer Hymnendichtung. O.R. Reisland.

21. Eco, U. (2004). History of Beauty. Rizzoli.

22. Elkins, J. (2004). On the Strange Place of Religion in Contemporary Art. Routledge.

23. Evdokimov, P. (1990). The Art of the Icon: A Theology of Beauty. Oakwood Publications.

24. Fassler, M. (2014). Music in the Medieval West. Norton.

25. Ferguson, K. (2002). Pythagoras: His Lives and the Legacy of a Rational Universe. Walker Publishing.

26. Francis. (2013). Evangelii gaudium [The Joy of the Gospel]. Vatican City: Vatican Press.

27. Gardner, H., Kleiner, F. S., & Mamiya, C. J. (2004). Gardner's art through the ages: The Western perspective. Thomson Wadsworth.

28. Hahn, S. (2009). The Lamb's Supper: The Mass as Heaven on Earth. Doubleday Religion.

29. Hildegard of Bingen. (n.d.). Music and Visions. Retrieved from http://www.hildegard.org/music/music.html

30. Hiley, D. (1993). Western Plainchant: A Handbook. Clarendon Press.

31. Jaki, S. L. (1986). The Savior of Science. Wm. B. Eerdmans Publishing Co.

32. Joffe, R. (Director). (1986). The Mission [Film]. Warner Bros.

33. John Paul II. (1990). Redemptoris missio. Vatican City: Libreria Editrice Vaticana.

34. John Paul II. (1998). Fides et Ratio: On the Relationship between Faith and Reason. Vatican City: Libreria Editrice Vaticana.

35. John Paul II. (1999). Letter to Artists. Vatican City: Libreria Editrice Vaticana.

36. Joncas, M. (2014). From sacred song to ritual music: Twentieth-century understandings of Roman Catholic worship music. Collegeville, MN: Liturgical Press.

37. Kelly, T. F. (2004). The Beneventan Chant. Cambridge University Press.

38. Kleinbauer, W. E. (2007). Modern perspectives in Western art history: An anthology of 20th-century writings on the visual arts. Medieval Academy of America.

39. Ladis, A. (1993). Giotto's O: Narrative, Figuration, and Pictorial Ingenuity in the Arena Chapel. Pennsylvania State University Press.

40. Leclercq, J. (1989). The Love of Learning and the Desire for God: A Study of Monastic Culture. Fordham University Press.

41. Lewis, K., & Sullivan, M. (2021). Saints and Their Symbols: Recognizing Saints in Art and in Popular Images. Loyola Press.

42. Maritain, J. (1943). Art and Scholasticism with Other Essays. Charles Scribner's Sons.

43. Matthew 25:14-30. (n.d.). The Parable of the Talents. New International Version Bible.

44. McDonnell, K. (1999). The Other Hand of God: The Holy Spirit as the Universal Touch and Goal. Collegeville, MN: Liturgical Press.

45. McInerny, R. (1998). Thomas Aquinas: Selected Writings. Penguin Classics.

46. New American Bible. (2011). United States Conference of Catholic Bishops.

47. Nichols, A. (1999). Redeeming Beauty: Soundings in Sacral Aesthetics. Farnham, Surrey: Ashgate.

48. O'Malley, W. (2015). Sacred Music and Liturgical Reform: Treasures and Transformations. Chicago: Liturgy Training Publications.

49. Ouspensky, L., & Lossky, V. (1982). The Meaning of Icons. Crestwood, NY: St. Vladimir's Seminary Press.

50. Paul II, J. (1998). Fides et Ratio. Libreria Editrice Vaticana.

51. Pieper, J. (1998). Leisure: The Basis of Culture. San Francisco: Ignatius Press.

52. Pieper, J. (2014). The Language of Liturgy: A Ritual Poetics. Liturgical Press.

53. Pope Benedict XVI. (2010). Verbum Domini. Vatican: The Holy See.

54. Pope Francis. (2013). Evangelii Gaudium [The Joy of the Gospel]. Vatican City: Libreria Editrice Vaticana.

55. Pope Francis. (2015). Laudato si': On Care for Our Common Home.

56. Pope Leo XIII. (1891). Rerum Novarum: Encyclical of Pope Leo XIII on Capital and Labor. Vatican.

57. Ratzinger, J. (2000). The Spirit of the Liturgy. San Francisco: Ignatius Press. Cardinal Ratzinger (Pope Benedict XVI) explores the deep connection between liturgy, art, and the New Evangelization, highlighting the essential role of beauty in drawing souls to God.

58. Ratzinger, J. (2000). The Spirit of the Liturgy. San Francisco: Ignatius Press.

59. Ratzinger, J. (2004). The Spirit of the Liturgy. San Francisco: Ignatius Press.

60. Rutter, J. (1985). Requiem [Album]. Hyperion Records.

61. Scarry, E. (1999). On Beauty and Being Just. Princeton, NJ: Princeton University Press.

62. Schmemann, A. (1986). The Eucharist: Sacrament of the Kingdom. St. Vladimir's Seminary Press.

63. Schoenauer, N. (1981). 6,000 Years of Housing. W.W. Norton & Company.

64. Sendler, E. (1988). The Icon: Image of the Invisible. Oakwood Publications.

65. Siedell, D. (2008). God in the gallery: A Christian embrace of modern art. Grand Rapids, MI: Baker Academic.

66. Steno, N. (1669). Dissertationis prodromus. Florence: Ex typographia sub signo Stellae.

67. Stroik, D. (2012). The Church Building as a Sacred Place: Beauty, Transcendence, and the Eternal. Chicago: Liturgy Training Publications.

68. Taruskin, R. (2010). The Oxford History of Western Music. Oxford University Press.

69. The Bible. (n.d.). The Holy Bible.

70. The Catechism of the Catholic Church. 2nd ed.,
Libreria Editrice Vaticana, 1997.

71. Thomas, G. (1996). Sacred Pathways. Zondervan.

72. United States Conference of Catholic Bishops.
(2020). Forming Consciences for Faithful Citizenship:
A Call to Political Responsibility.

73. Vasari, G. (1550). Lives of the Artists. Florence:
Giunti.

74. Vasari, G. (1550). Lives of the Most Excellent
Painters, Sculptors, and Architects. Florence: Lorenzo
Torrentino.

75. Vatican Council II. (1963). Inter Mirifica [Decree on
the Media of Social Communications]. Vatican City:
Libreria Editrice Vaticana.

76. Vatican Council II. (1963). Sacrosanctum concilium
[Constitution on the Sacred Liturgy]. Vatican City:
Vatican Press.

77. Vatican Council II. (1965). Gaudium et Spes. Vatican
City: Libreria Editrice Vaticana.

78. Vatican II. (1964). Lumen Gentium. Vatican: The
    Holy See.

79. Viladesau, R. (1999). The Beauty of the Cross: The
    Passion of Christ in Theology and the Arts from the
    Catacombs to the Eve of the Renaissance. Oxford,
    UK: Oxford University Press.

80. Viladesau, R. (1999). Theological Aesthetics: God in
    Imagination, Beauty, and Art. Oxford University
    Press.

81. Viladesau, R. (2000). Theology and the Arts:
    Encountering God through Music, Art and
    Architecture. New York: Paulist Press.

82. Vogel, C. (1990). Medieval Liturgy: An Introduction
    to the Sources. Pastoral Press.

83. Von Balthasar, H. U. (1982). The Glory of the Lord:
    A Theological Aesthetics, Vol. 1, Seeing the Form.
    San Francisco: Ignatius Press.

84. Von Balthasar, H. U. (1982). The Glory of the Lord:
    A Theological Aesthetics. Edinburgh: T&T Clark.

85. Wallace, D. (2015). Saints and their lives: On the periphery of historiography. Church History, 84(2), 300-312.

86. Ware, T. (1993). The Orthodox Church: An Introduction to its History, Doctrine, and Spiritual Culture. Penguin Books.

87. Weisheipl, J. A. (1983). Friar Thomas d'Aquino: His Life, Thought, and Works. Catholic University of America Press.

88. Wilson-Dickson, A. (1992). The Story of Christian Music. Augsburg Fortress.

89. Woods, T. (2005). How the Catholic Church Built Western Civilization. Regnery Publishing.

THE 15 PRAYERS OF ST. BRIDGET

These Prayers and these Promises have been copied from a book printed in Toulouse in 1740 and published by the P. Adrien Parvilliers of the Company of Jesus, Apostolic Missionary of the Holy Land, with approbation, permission and recommendation to distribute them.

Pope Pius IX took cognisance of these Prayers with the prologue; he approved them May 31, 1862, recognising them as true and for the good of souls.

As St. Bridget for a long time wanted to know the number of blows Our Lord received during His Passion, He one day appeared to her and said: "I received 5480 blows on My Body. If you wish to honour them in some way, say 15 Our Fathers and 15 Hail Marys with the following Prayers (which He taught her) for a whole year. When the year is up, you will have honoured each one of My Wounds."

He made the following promises to anyone who recited these Prayers for a whole year:

1. I will deliver 15 souls of his lineage from Purgatory.

2. 15 souls of his lineage will be confirmed and preserved in grace.

3.   15 sinners of his lineage will be converted.

4.   Whoever recites these Prayers will attain the first degree of perfection.

5.   15 days before his death I will give him My Precious Body in order that he may escape eternal starvation; I will give him My Precious Blood to drink lest he thirst eternally.

6.   15 days before his death he will feel a deep contrition for all his sins and will have a perfect knowledge of them.

7.   I will place before him the sign of My Victorious Cross for his help and defence against the attacks of his enemies.

8.   Before his death I shall come with My Dearest Beloved Mother.

9.   I shall graciously receive his soul, and will lead it into eternal joys.

10. And having led it there I shall give him a special draught from the fountain of My Deity, something I will not for those who have not recited My Prayers.

11. Let it be known that whoever may have been living in a state of mortal sin for 30 years, but who will recite

devoutly, or have the intention to recite these Prayers, the Lord will forgive him all his sins.

12. I shall protect him from strong temptations.

13. I shall preserve and guard his 5 senses.

14. I shall preserve him from a sudden death.

15. His soul will be delivered from eternal death.

16. He will obtain all he asks for from God and the Blessed Virgin.

17. If he has lived all his life doing his own will and he is to die the next day, his life will be prolonged.

18. Every time one recites these Prayers he gains 100 days indulgence.

19. He is assured of being joined to the supreme Choir of Angels.

20. Whoever teaches these Prayers to another, will have continuous joy and merit which will endure eternally.

21. There where these Prayers are being said or will be said in the future God is present with His grace.

Each prayer is preceded by one Our Father and one Hail Mary.

Our Father, who art in heaven, hallowed be thy name.
Thy kingdom come.
Thy will be done on earth as it is in heaven.
Give us this day our daily bread and forgive us our trespasses as we
forgive those who trespass against us and lead us not into temptation
but deliver us from evil. **Amen**

Hail Mary, full of grace, the Lord is with thee; blessed art thou
among women and blessed is the fruit of thy womb, Jesus.
Holy Mary, Mother of God, pray for us sinners, now and at the hour
of our death. **Amen.**

FIRST PRAYER
Our Father – Hail Mary.
O Jesus Christ! Eternal Sweetness to those who love Thee, joy
surpassing all joy and all desire, Salvation and Hope of all sinners,
Who hast proved that Thou hast no greater desire than to be among
men, even assuming human nature at the fullness of time for the
love of men, recall all the sufferings Thou hast endured from the
instant of Thy conception, and especially during Thy Passion, as it
was decreed and ordained from all eternity in the Divine plan.

Remember, O Lord, that during the Last Supper with Thy disciples, having washed their feet, Thou gavest them Thy Most Precious Body and Blood, and while at the same time thou didst sweetly console them, Thou didst foretell them Thy coming Passion. Remember the sadness and bitterness which Thou didst experience in Thy Soul as Thou Thyself bore witness saying: "My Soul is sorrowful even unto death."

Remember all the fear, anguish and pain that Thou didst suffer in Thy delicate Body before the torment of the Crucifixion, when, after having prayed three times, bathed in a sweat of blood, Thou wast betrayed by Judas, Thy disciple, arrested by the people of a nation Thou hadst chosen and elevated, accused by false witnesses, unjustly judged by three judges during the flower of Thy youth and during the solemn Paschal season.

Remember that Thou wast despoiled of Thy garments and clothed in those of derision; that Thy Face and Eyes were veiled, that Thou wast buffeted, crowned with thorns, a reed placed in Thy Hands, that Thou was crushed with blows and overwhelmed with affronts and outrages.
In memory of all these pains and sufferings which Thou didst endure before Thy Passion on the Cross, grant me before my death true contrition, a sincere and entire confession, worthy satisfaction and the remission of all my sins. **Amen.**

SECOND PRAYER

Our Father – Hail Mary.

O Jesus! True liberty of angels, Paradise of delights, remember the horror and sadness which Thou didst endure when Thy enemies, like furious lions, surrounded Thee, and by thousands of insults, spits, blows, lacerations and other unheard-of-cruelties, tormented Thee at will.

In consideration of these torments and insulting words, I beseech Thee, O my Saviour, to deliver me from all my enemies, visible and invisible, and to bring me, under Thy protection, to the perfection of eternal salvation. **Amen.**

THIRD PRAYER

Our Father – Hail Mary.

O Jesus! Creator of Heaven and earth Whom nothing can encompass or limit, Thou Who dost enfold and hold all under Thy Loving power, remember the very bitter pain.

Thou didst suffer when the Jews nailed Thy Sacred Hands and Feet to the Cross by blow after blow with big blunt nails, and not finding Thee in a pitiable enough state to satisfy their rage, they enlarged Thy Wounds, and added pain to pain, and with indescribable cruelty stretched Thy Body
on the Cross, pulled Thee from all sides, thus dislocating Thy

Limbs.

I beg of Thee, O Jesus, by the memory of this most Loving suffering of the Cross, to grant me the grace to fear Thee and to Love Thee. **Amen.**

FOURTH PRAYER

Our Father – Hail Mary.

O Jesus! Heavenly Physician, raised aloft on the Cross to heal our wounds with Thine, remember the bruises which Thou didst suffer and the weakness of all Thy Members which were distended to such a degree that never was there pain like unto Thine.

From the crown of Thy Head to the Soles of Thy Feet there was not one spot on Thy Body that was not in torment, and yet, forgetting all Thy sufferings, Thou didst not cease to pray to Thy Heavenly Father for Thy enemies, saying: "Father forgive them for they know not what they do."

Through this great Mercy, and in memory of this suffering, grant that the remembrance of Thy Most Bitter Passion may effect in us a perfect contrition and the remission of all our sins. **Amen.**

FIFTH PRAYER

Our Father – Hail Mary.

O Jesus! Mirror of eternal splendour, remember the sadness which Thou experienced, when contemplating in the light of Thy Divinity the predestination of those who would be saved by the merits of Thy Sacred Passion.

Thou didst see at the same time, the great multitude of reprobates who would be damned for their sins, and Thou didst complain bitterly of those hopeless lost and unfortunate sinners.

Through this abyss of compassion and pity, and especially through the goodness which Thou displayed to the good thief when Thou saidst to him: "This day, thou shalt be with Me in Paradise." I beg of Thee, O Sweet Jesus, that at the hour of my death, Thou wilt show me mercy. **Amen.**

SIXTH PRAYER

Our Father – Hail Mary.

O Jesus! Beloved and most desirable King, remember the grief Thou didst suffer, when naked and like a common criminal.

Thou was fastened and raised on the Cross, when all Thy relatives and friends abandoned Thee, except Thy Beloved Mother, who remained close to Thee during Thy agony and whom Thou didst entrust to Thy faithful disciple when Thou saidst to Mary: "Woman, behold thy son!" and to St. John: "Son, behold thy Mother!"

I beg of Thee O my Saviour, by the sword of sorrow which pierced the soul of Thy holy Mother, to have compassion on me in all my affliction and tribulations, both corporal and spiritual, and to assist me in all my trials, and especially at the hour of my death. **Amen**.

SEVENTH PRAYER

Our Father – Hail Mary.

O Jesus! Inexhaustible Fountain of compassion, Who by a profound gesture of Love, said from the Cross: "I thirst!" suffered from the thirst for the salvation of the human race.

I beg of Thee O my Saviour, to inflame in our hearts the desire to tend toward perfection in all our acts; and to extinguish in us the concupiscence of the flesh and the ardor of worldly desires. **Amen**.

EIGHTH PRAYER

Our Father – Hail Mary.

O Jesus! Sweetness of hearts, delight of the spirit, by the bitterness of the vinegar and gall which Thou didst taste on the Cross for Love of us, grant us the grace to receive worthily.

Thy Precious Body and Blood during our life and at the hour of our death, that they may serve as a remedy and consolation for our souls. **Amen.**

NINTH PRAYER

Our Father – Hail Mary.

O Jesus! Royal virtue, joy of the mind, recall the pain Thou didst endure when, plunged in an ocean of bitterness at the approach of death, insulted, outraged by the Jews.

Thou didst cry out in a loud voice that Thou was abandoned by Thy Father, saying: "My God, My God, why hast Thou forsaken me?"

Through this anguish, I beg of Thee, O my Saviour, not to abandon me in the terrors and pains of my death. **Amen.**

TENTH PRAYER

Our Father – Hail Mary.

O Jesus! Who art the beginning and end of all things, life and virtue, remembers that for our sakes Thou was plunged in an abyss of suffering from the soles of Thy Feet to the crown of Thy Head.

In consideration of the enormity of Thy Wounds, teach me to keep, through pure love, Thy Commandments, whose way is wide and easy for those who love Thee. **Amen.**

ELEVENTH PRAYER

Our Father – Hail Mary.

O Jesus! Deep abyss of mercy, I beg of Thee, in memory of Thy Wounds which penetrated to the very marrow of Thy Bones and to the depth of Thy being, to draw me, a miserable sinner, overwhelmed by my offenses, away from sin and to hide me from Thy Face justly irritated against me, hide me in Thy wounds, until Thy anger and just indignation shall have passed away. **Amen.**

TWELFTH PRAYER

Our Father – Hail Mary.

O Jesus! Mirror of Truth, symbol of unity, bond of charity, remember the multitude of wounds with which Thou wast afflicted from head to foot, torn and reddened by the spilling of Thy adorable Blood. O great and universal pain, which Thou didst suffer in Thy virginal flesh for love of us! Sweetest Jesus! What is there that Thou couldst have done for us which Thou has not done!

May the fruit of Thy suffering be renewed in my soul by the faithful remembrance of Thy Passion, and may Thy love increase in my heart each day, until I see Thee in eternity: Thou Who art the treasure of every real good and every joy, which I beg Thee to grant me, O Sweetest Jesus, in heaven. **Amen.**

THIRTEENTH PRAYER

Our Father – Hail Mary.

O Jesus! Strong Lion, Immortal and Invincible King, remember the pain which Thou didst endure when all Thy strength, both moral and physical, was entirely exhausted, Thou didst bow Thy Head, saying: "It is consummated!"

Through this anguish and grief, I beg of Thee Lord Jesus, to have mercy on me at the hour of my death when my mind will be greatly troubled and my soul will be in anguish. **Amen.**

FOURTEENTH PRAYER

Our Father – Hail Mary.

O Jesus! Only Son of the Father, Splendour and Figure of His Substance, remember the simple and humble recommendation.

Thou didst make of Thy Soul to Thy Eternal Father, saying: "Father, into Thy Hands I commend My Spirit!" And with Thy Body all torn, and Thy Heart Broken, and the bowels of Thy Mercy open to redeem us, Thou didst Expire.

By this Precious Death, I beg of Thee O King of Saints, comfort me and help me to resist the devil, the flesh and the world, so that being dead to the world I may live for Thee alone.

I beg of Thee at the hour of my death to receive me, a pilgrim and an exile returning to Thee. **Amen.**

FIFTEENTH PRAYER

Our Father – Hail Mary.

O Jesus! True and fruitful Vine! Remember the abundant outpouring of Blood which Thou didst so generously shed from Thy Sacred Body as juice from grapes in a wine press.

From Thy Side, pierced with a lance by a soldier, blood and water issued forth until there was not left in Thy Body a single drop, and finally, like a bundle of myrrh lifted to the top of the Cross Thy delicate Flesh was destroyed, the very Substance of Thy Body withered, and the Marrow of Thy Bones dried up.

Through this bitter Passion and through the outpouring of Thy Precious Blood, I beg of Thee, O Sweet Jesus, to receive my soul when I am in my death agony. **Amen.**

CONCLUSION

O Sweet Jesus! Pierce my heart so that my tears of penitence and love will be my bread day and night; may I be converted entirely to

Thee, may my heart be Thy perpetual habitation, may my conversation be pleasing to Thee, and may the end of my life be so praiseworthy that I may merit Heaven and there with Thy saints, praise Thee forever. **Amen.**